Crush the CogAT® Series
Practice Test 1

Grades K, 1 and 2

by Big Brains Books

Printed in the United States of America

Table of Contents

Introduction

The *Cognitive Abilities Test*®(CogAT®) is a multi-battery test intended to measure reasoning and problem-solving skills in three areas: verbal, nonverbal, and quantitative. It is often given with the *Iowa Test of Basic Skills*® (ITBS®) to also assess student achievement. In particular, it is often employed to evaluate whether students in grades K through 8 should be placed into accelerated learning programs. Standards vary depending on the school district, but an excellent score on this exam is often the first step toward acceptance into these special programs.

While the test itself is not difficult, questions are posed in ways that differ from conventional testing. The test authors and the districts that use the CogAT® to screen for "giftedness" believe that appropriately gifted children will be able to adapt during the testing process, our experience is that the standards adopted by most districts are so stringent that even one or two mistakes can eliminate a student from qualification for accelerated learning programs. Understandably, even the most capable students will make mistakes when presented with tricky, new material. As a result, we at Big Brains Books have been developing materials for more than a decade to provide familiarity and practice with questions that are similar in structure and difficulty to those appearing on the CogAT®.

We have designed our practice tests and strategy guide (*Crush the CogAT*®) specifically to help your child qualify for your district's accelerated learning program. We believe that our practice tests and our strategy guide will provide familiarity with the test and approaches to the questions that will promote optimal performance.

Tips

What everyone says (Good advice, but not very helpful…):

Get a good night's sleep

Ensure a good night's sleep. According to Dr. Robert Oexman, the director of the Sleep to Live Institute, sleeping before a big test is as effective as studying an additional four or five hours. Being well rested also helps with concentration, which is a primary concern when testing young children. The night before the test, make sure your student gets a full eight or more hours of sleep.

Eat well

Make sure your student is well fed in the morning: minimal sugar, lots of protein. As for a snack, avoid candy or sweet energy bars; rather, send healthier options like peanut butter and celery sticks, yogurt with nuts and fruit, or even baby carrots with cream cheese. Always pack water. You don't want your child focused on the next snack break instead of the test.

Listen to the instructions

Even with the practice from this book, make sure your child knows to pay attention to all the instructions to avoid any surprises on the test and make sure they listen to all of the instructions before beginning.

Don't look at the answers right away

Test-takers should try figuring out what the answer **should be** before looking at the answer choices. They won't always come up with the correct answer, but thinking about what the answer SHOULD be will encourage critical thinking about the question. (More on this critical skill in *Crush the CogAT®*)

Read all options

Even if the correct answer seems apparent, urge your child to examine all answer choices before making a final decision. CogAT® questions will often include more than one possible answer, so it is up to the test-taker to determine which answer is best. In these cases, only by examining the question more carefully can the clues for the correct answer be determined.

Eliminate wrong answers

In cases when the test-taker is unsure of the correct answer, eliminate the answers that are definitely wrong. Process Of Elimination (POE) can be an effective strategy, especially when faced with unfamiliar quantitative problems or unknown vocabulary.

Always guess if you don't know the answer

There is no guessing penalty, so never leave a question blank. (Although, if you've properly prepared with a strategy for each type of question, you should NEVER have to guess randomly.)

Color the bubble fully

The test is machine-evaluated, so test bubbles that have been inadequately filled in will not be read.

...better tips!

(A subset of the information and strategies presented in our book *Crush the CogAT®*)

Find a strategy and use it!

For each type of question, you should have one strategy. A way of solving it that ALWAYS works. Each time you answer a question, you should be able to say exactly WHY your answer is correct. In the following example, a table GOES WITH a chair just as a hamburger GOES WITH a bun. There is NO other answer where GOES WITH works.

Focus on weaknesses

When using this book, see which types of questions your student is not answering correctly and focus on those areas. Specifically, work on the strategy for those sections.

Practice, practice, practice

As with all things, familiarity comes with repetition. We are big fans of this teaching strategy. Ideally you'll be able to purchase all three of our practice tests (and use copies of the included answer forms) to provide plenty of practice. However, even with just this one test, students can repeat the test (that IS why we provide answer forms), can practice by creating their own questions based on ours (we'd love to see your creations! email them to creations@bigbrainsbooks.com), and can practice using new strategies to solve the problems (some of our best discussions with students have come from discussing why certain strategies sometimes work and sometimes don't). Start early and do a little practice every day, but don't do marathon sessions. Your child will hate them and not learn as much as when you engage in multiple, brief sessions.

We've included separate answer sheets for each test in the book. We highly recommend copying them and allowing your student to take the tests multiple times. With repetition, the focus is less on finding the correct answer and more on practicing the logic necessary to find the right answer. Asking "Why is this the right answer?" when they make their selection will allow you to make sure they are thinking about the questions rather than simply "going through the motions."

Crush the CogAT® Series
Practice Test 1

Grades K, 1 and 2

BIG
BRAINS
BOOKS

Directions:

The questions in this section are like the sample below:

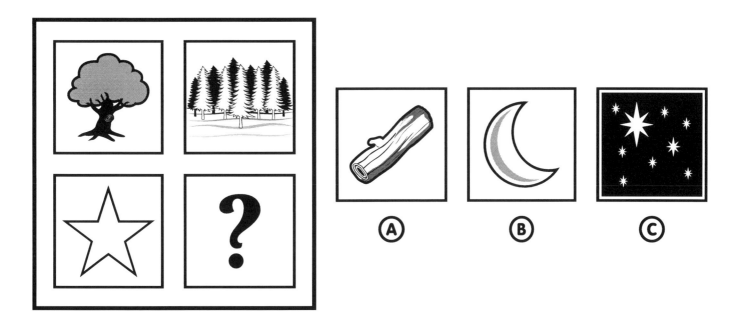

Look at the top two pictures. Think about how they are related (Are they the same? Are they different in some particular way? Are they used for the same thing?). Now look at the lower picture. Which of the answer choices belongs with the lower picture, the same way that the two upper pictures belong together? A **tree** is part of a **forest** just like a **star** is part of a **night sky** (one to many/one to many).

Find the area marked Picture Analogies on your answer sheet. Now find the S (sample) row. Since the answer is **night sky**, fill in the **C** space in row S.

Do all of the questions in this section in the same way (using the bubbles under each question or on the answer sheets, as your parents want). Try to answer each question.

Picture Analogies

1.

(A)

(B)

(C)

2.

(F)

(G)

(H)

3.

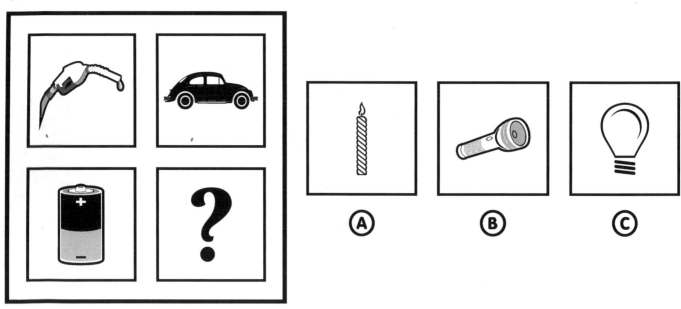

4.

5.

6.

7.

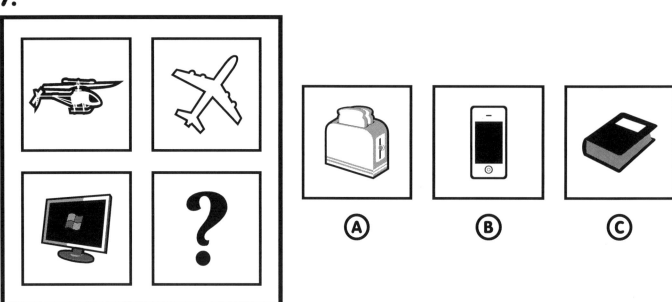

8.

Picture Analogies

9.

(A)

(B)

(C)

10.

(F)

(G)

(H)

Picture Analogies

11.

12.

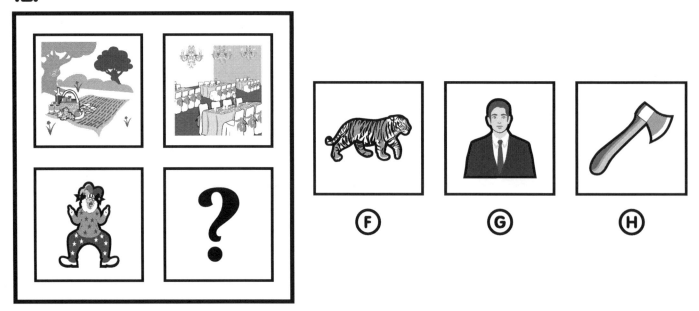

Picture Analogies

13.

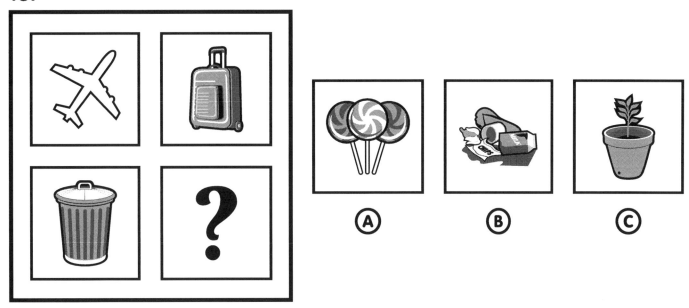

14.

Picture Analogies

15.

Ⓐ   Ⓑ   Ⓒ

16.

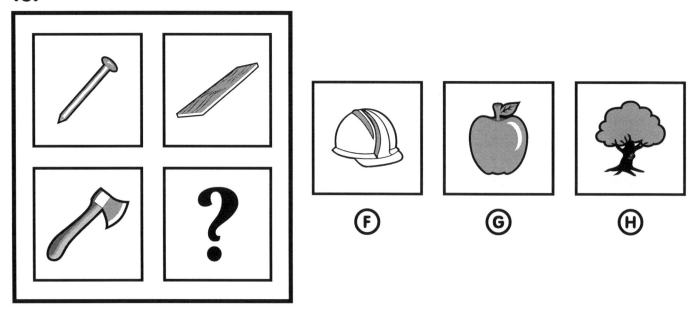

Ⓕ   Ⓖ   Ⓗ

17.

18.

Directions:

(These questions will be read to the student during the actual test. Feel free to read the questions to your student if she is struggling with reading them herself.)

The questions in this section are like the sample below:

The _____ is renowned for its ability to survive in the desert.

Ⓐ Ⓑ Ⓒ Ⓓ Ⓔ

Read (Listen to) the sentence. Then read (listen to) the answer choices and find the word that makes the most sense in the blank. Each sentence will contain a "clue" that helps you find one most correct answer. In this sentence the clue is **desert**, so the answer is obviously **camel**.

Find the area marked Sentence Completion on your answer sheet. Now find the S (sample) row. Since the answer is **camel**, fill in the **B** space in row S.

Do all of the questions in this section in the same way (using the bubbles under each question or on the answer sheets, as your parents want). Try to answer each question.

1. Which of these could roll down a hill?

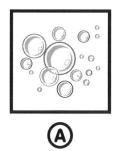
(A)

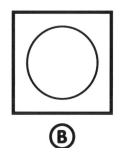
(B)

(C)

(D)

(E)

2. What did Jose hit with his racket?

(F)

(G)

(H)

(I)

(J)

3. At midnight, which is large and bright?

(A)

(B)

(C)

(D)

(E)

4. Next to the school, we play soccer here.

(F)

(G)

(H)

(I)

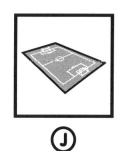
(J)

5. In order to travel from New York to Los Angeles, where did Zane go?

Ⓐ Ⓑ Ⓒ Ⓓ Ⓔ

6. Where do most people carry their money?

Ⓕ Ⓖ Ⓗ Ⓘ Ⓙ

7. What did she leave in the parking lot outside the supermarket?

Ⓐ Ⓑ Ⓒ Ⓓ Ⓔ

8. Kelsey wandered around her school until she got a call on her _____.

Ⓕ Ⓖ Ⓗ Ⓘ Ⓙ

9. What do you tie on top of a present?

   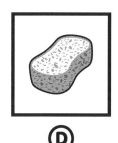 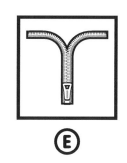

Ⓐ Ⓑ Ⓒ Ⓓ Ⓔ

10. Would you like a _____ of juice?

Ⓕ Ⓖ Ⓗ Ⓘ Ⓙ

11. What grows on vines?

Ⓐ Ⓑ Ⓒ Ⓓ Ⓔ

12. Which has petals that wilt without water?

   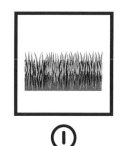 

Ⓕ Ⓖ Ⓗ Ⓘ Ⓙ

13. What did Isabelle break that kept her from finishing her report?

(A)　　(B)　　(C)　　(D)　　(E)

14. What do we use to be heard by everyone in a stadium?

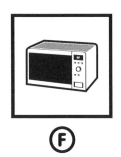    

(F)　　(G)　　(H)　　(I)　　(J)

15. At the end of day, which of these sets?

(A)　　(B)　　(C)　　(D)　　(E)

16. The meeting was rudely interrupted by the beeping of the _____.

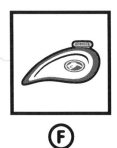    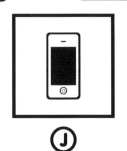

(F)　　(G)　　(H)　　(I)　　(J)

17. **What animal is known for its size, speed and strength?**

Ⓐ   Ⓑ   Ⓒ   Ⓓ   Ⓔ

18. **After jumping into the _____, Luke's mouth was filled with the taste of salt.**

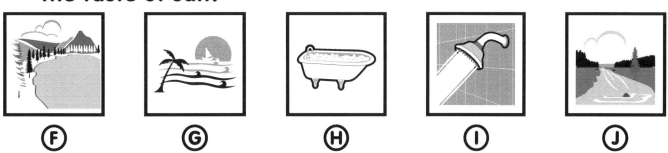

Ⓕ   Ⓖ   Ⓗ   Ⓘ   Ⓙ

Directions:

The questions in this section are like the sample below:

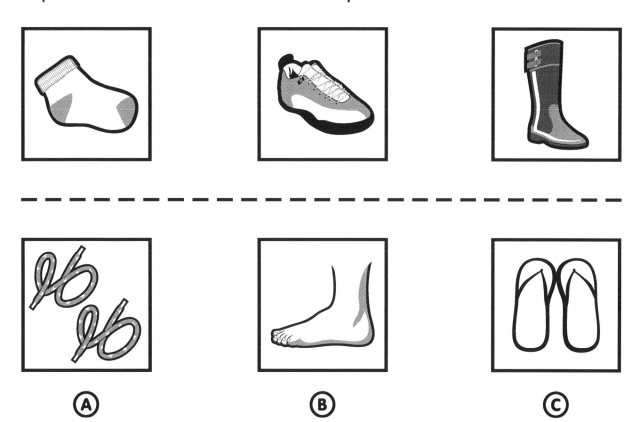

(A)   (B)   (C)

Look at the top three pictures. Think about how they are the same. Now look at the answer choices and find the choice that belongs in the same group (that is the same in the same way). A **sock, a sneaker and a boot** are all things that go on your feet; just like flip flops do.

Find the area marked Picture Classification on your answer sheet. Now find the S (sample) row. Since the answer is **flip flops**, fill in the **C** space in row S.

Do all of the questions in this section in the same way (using the bubbles under each question or on the answer sheets, as your parents want). Try to answer each question.

Picture Classification

1.

(A)   (B)   (C)

2.

(F)   (G)   (H)

3.

(A) (B) (C)

4.

(F) (G) (H)

5.

Ⓐ   Ⓑ   Ⓒ

6.

Ⓕ   Ⓖ   Ⓗ

7.

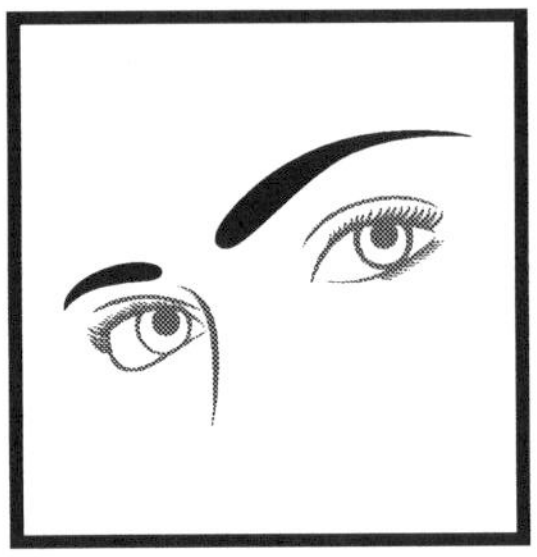

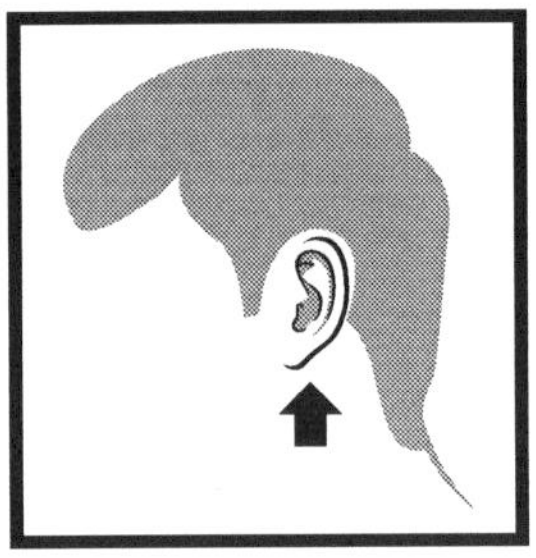

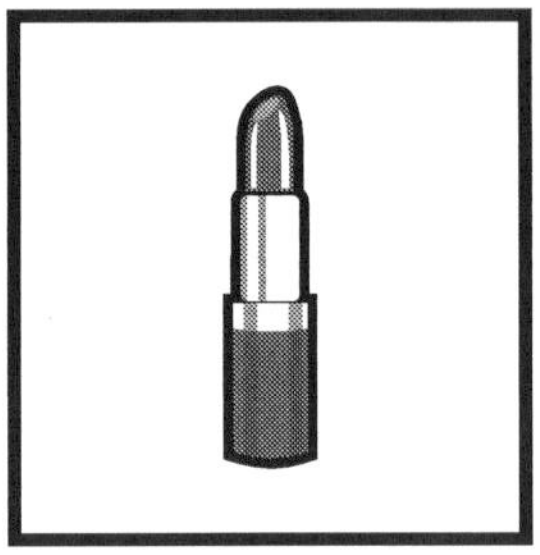

A

B

C

8.

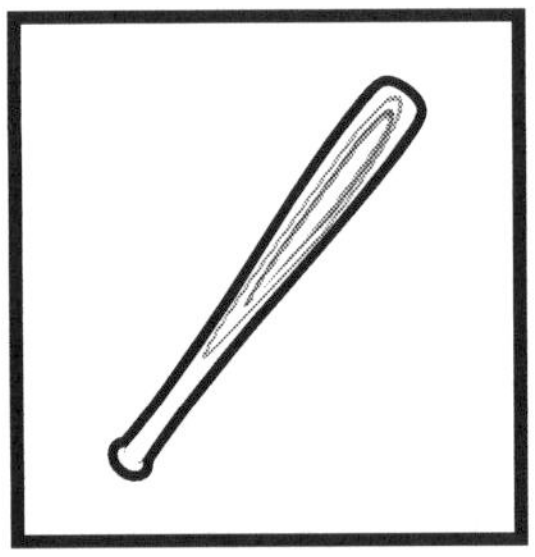

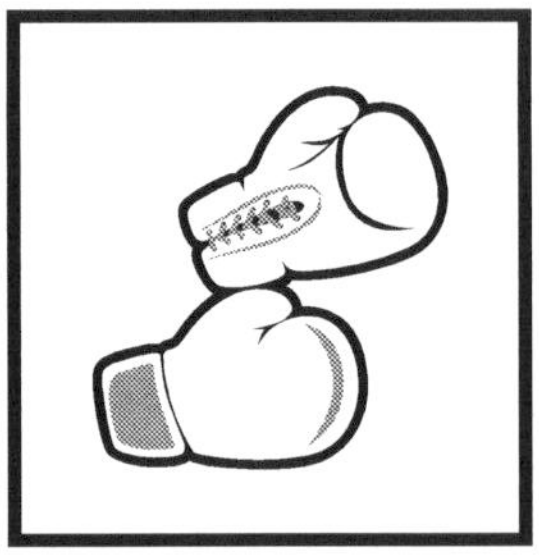

F

G

H

Picture Classification

9.

- -

Ⓐ

Ⓑ

Ⓒ

10.

- -

Ⓕ

Ⓖ

Ⓗ

11.

(A)   (B)   (C)

12.

(F)   (G)   (H)

13.

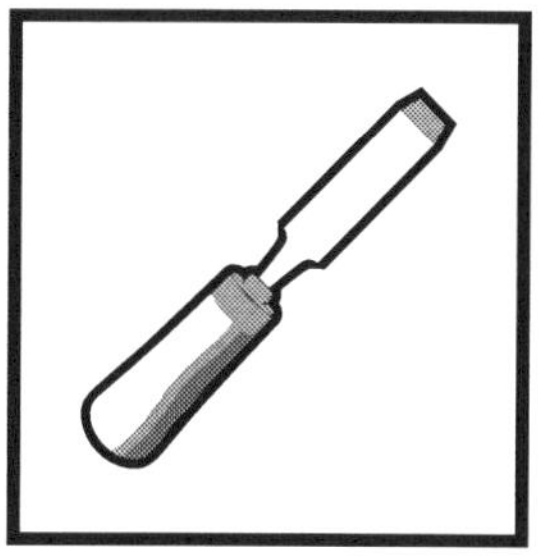

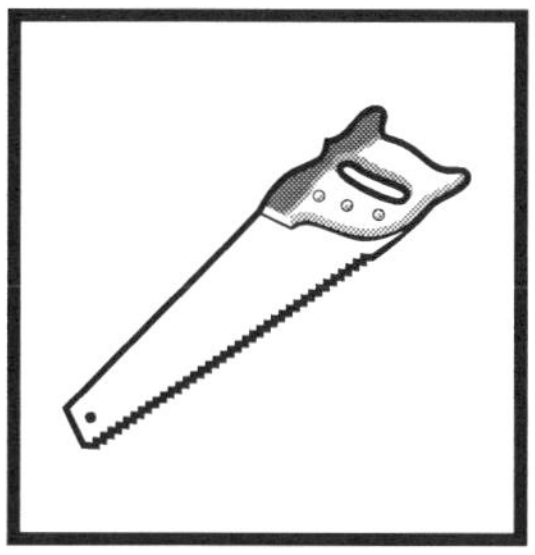

Ⓐ

Ⓑ

Ⓒ

14.

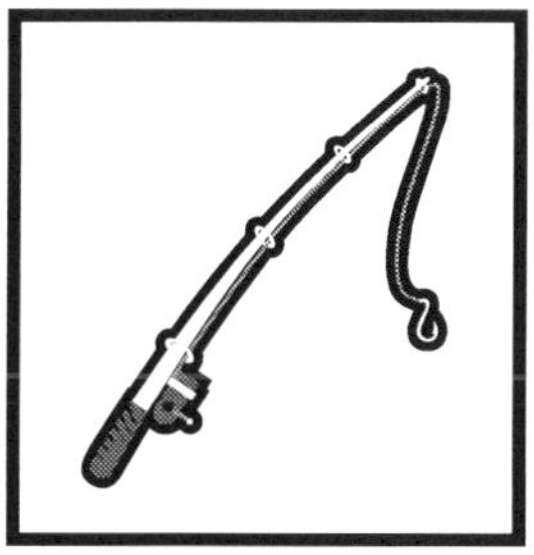

Ⓕ

Ⓖ

Ⓗ

15.

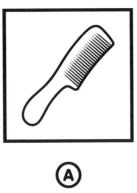

Ⓐ Ⓑ Ⓒ

16.

Ⓕ Ⓖ Ⓗ

Picture Classification

17.

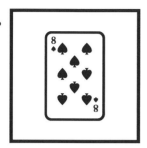  

(A)   (B)   (C)

18.

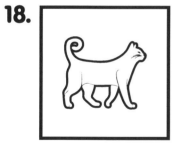  

(F)   (G)   (H)

Directions:

The questions in this section are like the sample below:

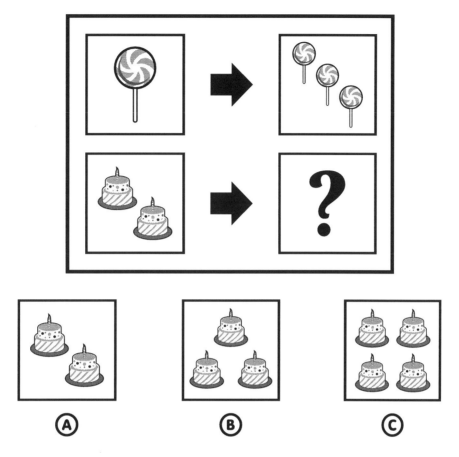

Look at the top two pictures. Each one represents a number. Think about how those numbers are related. In this case, **adding two** to the first number gives the second. Now look at the lower picture. Which of the answer choices creates the same relationship with the lower picture, as the two upper pictures have together? Clearly, **adding two** to two gives **four**. So the correct answer would be **C**.

Find the area marked Number Analogies on your answer sheet. Now find the S (sample) row. Since the answer is **4**, fill in the **C** space in row S.

Do all of the questions in this section in the same way (using the bubbles under each question or on the answer sheets, as your parents want). Try to answer each question.

Number Analogies

1.

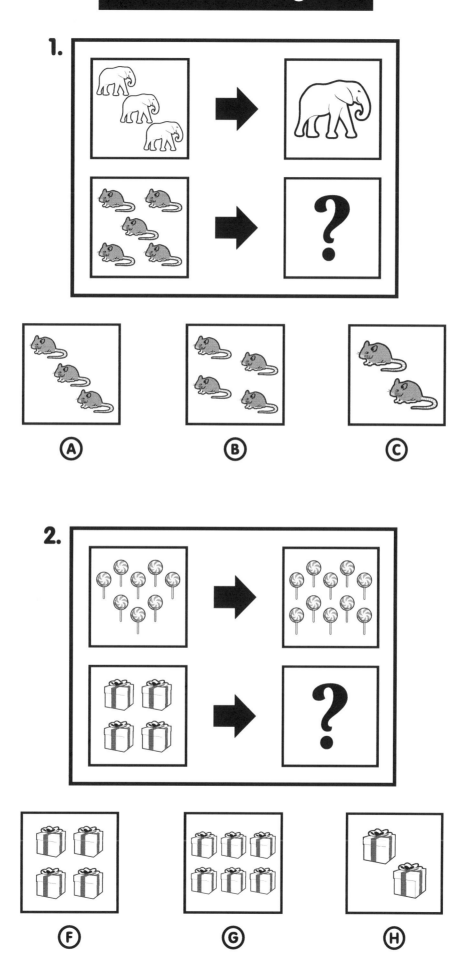

Number Analogies

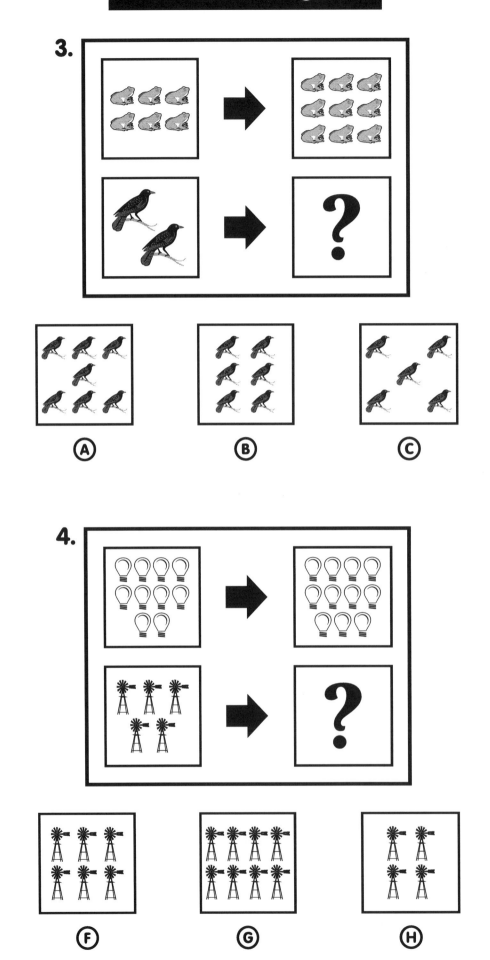

Big Brains Books - Crush the CogAT® Series - Practice Test 1

Number Analogies

5.

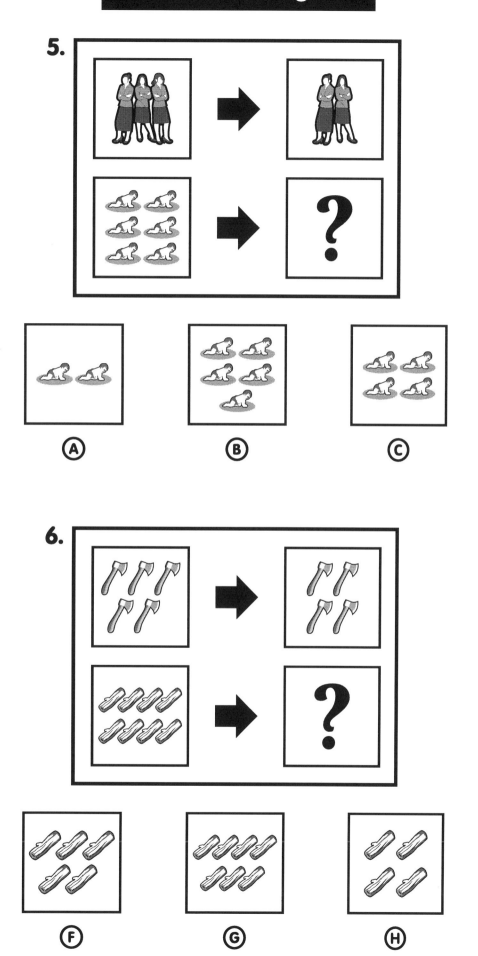

Ⓐ   Ⓑ   Ⓒ

6.

Ⓕ   Ⓖ   Ⓗ

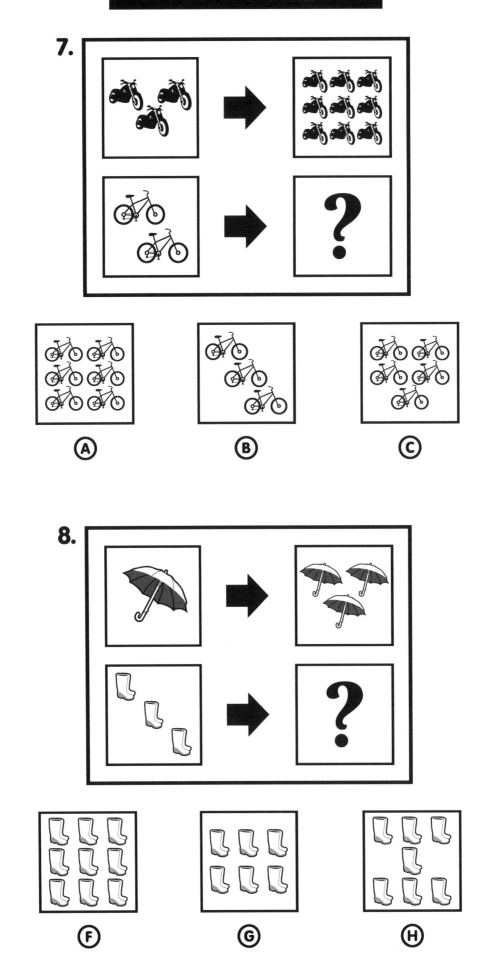

7.

A

B

C

8.

F

G

H

Number Analogies

9.

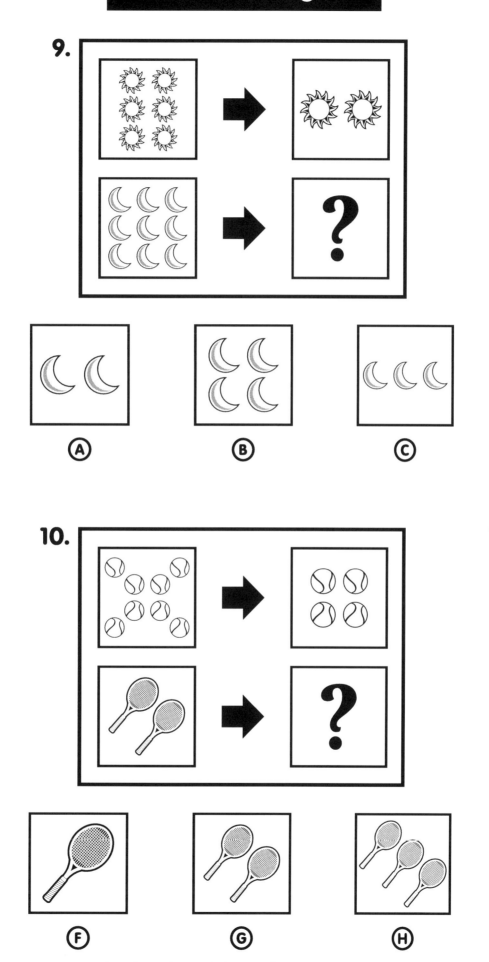

Ⓐ   Ⓑ   Ⓒ

10.

Ⓕ   Ⓖ   Ⓗ

Number Analogies

11.

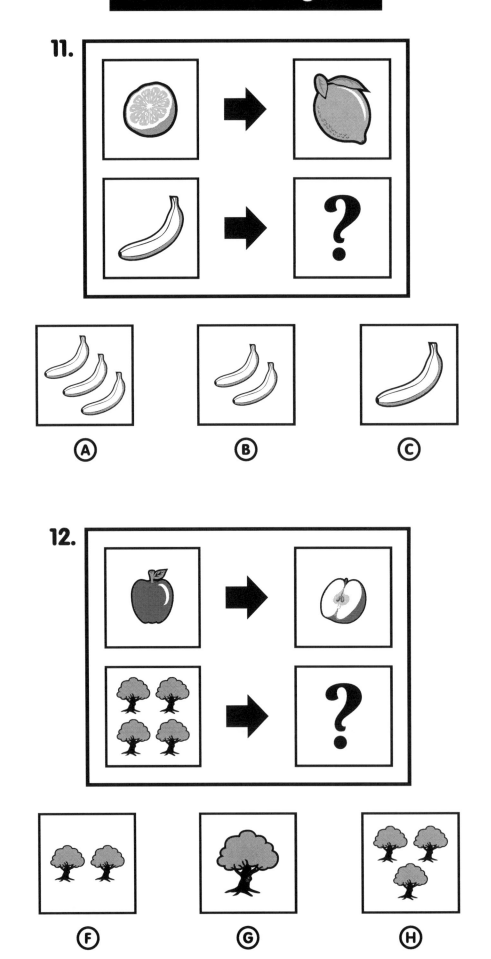

A   B   C

12.

F   G   H

Number Analogies

13.

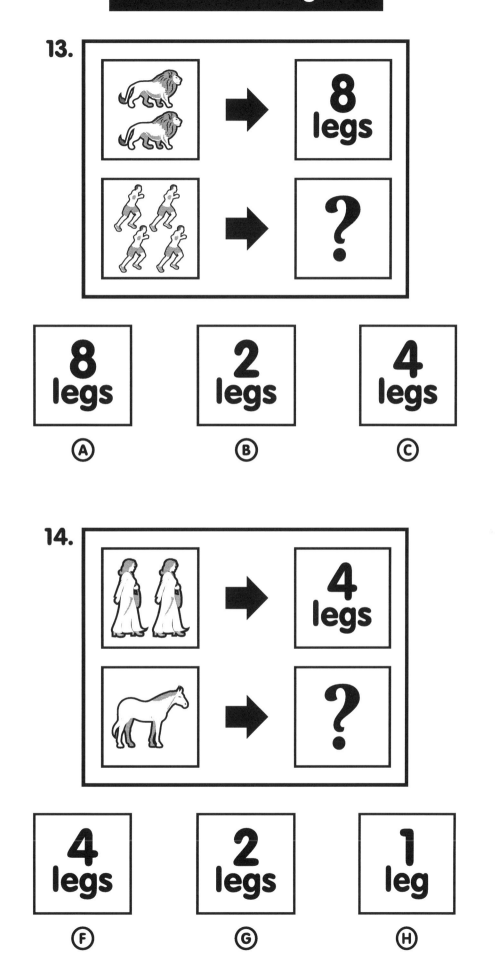

8 legs
(A)

2 legs
(B)

4 legs
(C)

14.

4 legs
(F)

2 legs
(G)

1 leg
(H)

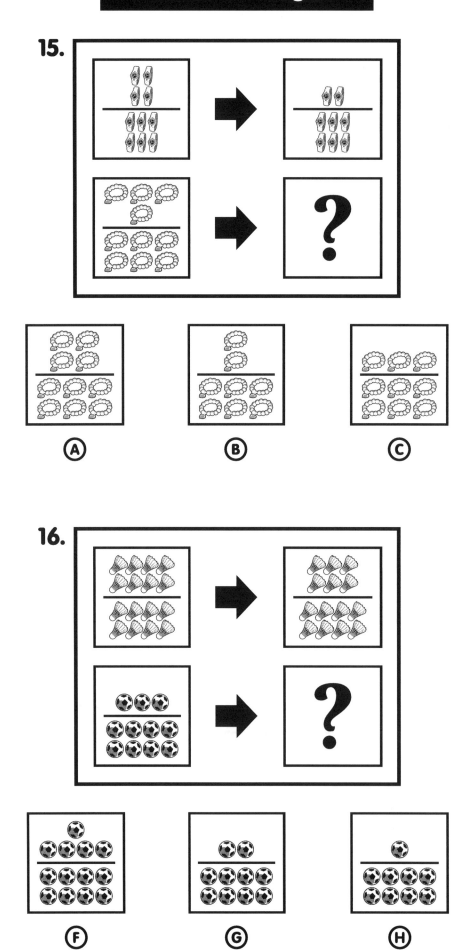

15.

A   B   C

16.

F   G   H

17.

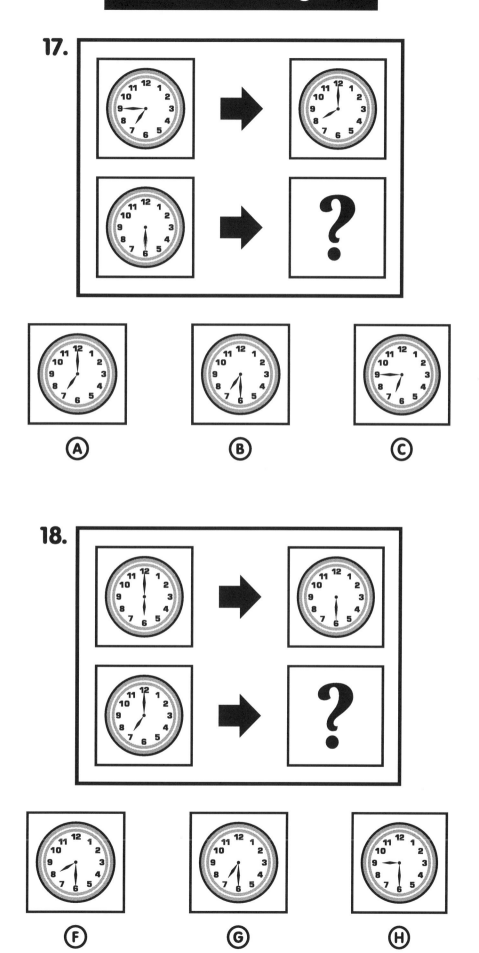

Ⓐ   Ⓑ   Ⓒ

18.

Ⓕ   Ⓖ   Ⓗ

Directions:

The questions in this section are like the sample below:

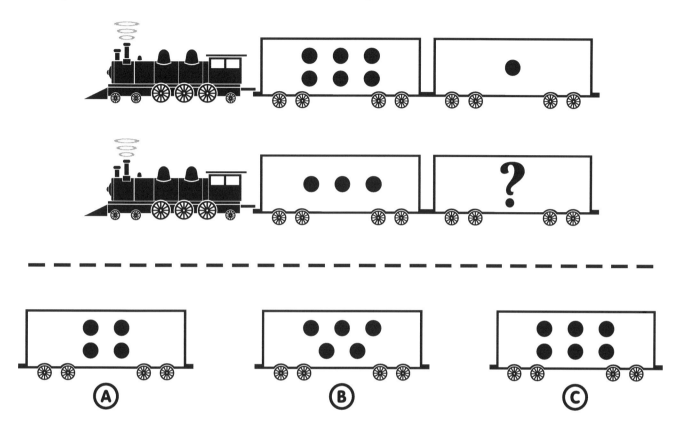

Look at the top picture of the train. Think about how many total items are on the train cars. Now look at the lower train and the answer choices. Choose the answer choice that will make the number of items on the lower train equal to the number of items on the upper train. Since the upper train has **7 total items** and the lower train has **3 items**, we need to add **4 items** to make the two have the same number of items.

Find the area marked Number Puzzles on your answer sheet. Now find the S (sample) row. Since the answer is **4**, fill in the **A** space in row S.

Do all of the questions in this section in the same way (using the bubbles under each question or on the answer sheets, as your parents want). Try to answer each question.

1.

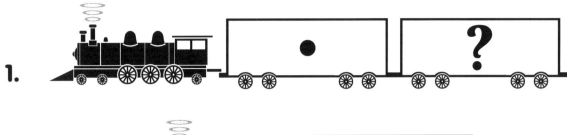

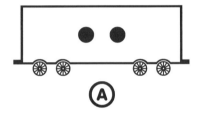

(A)

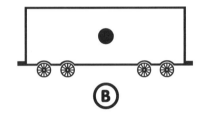

(B)

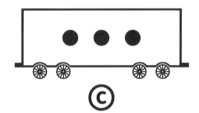

(C)

2.

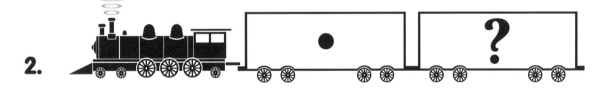

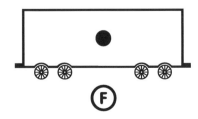

(F)

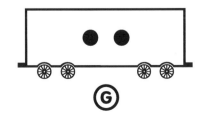

(G)

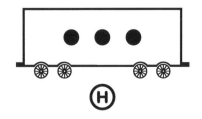

(H)

3.

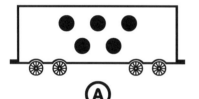

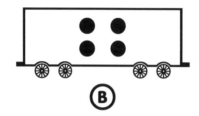 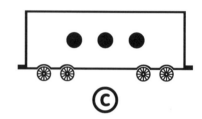

(A) (B) (C)

4.

(F) (G) (H)

5.

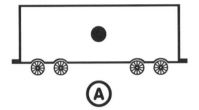

(A)

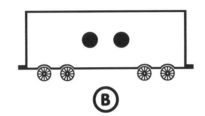

(B)

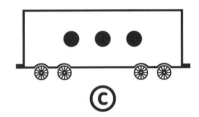

(C)

6.

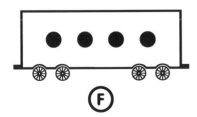

(F)

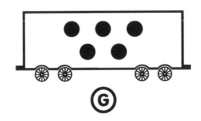

(G)

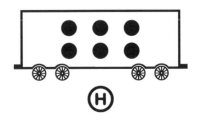

(H)

7.

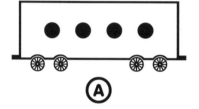

(A)

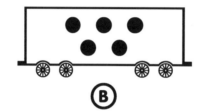

(B)

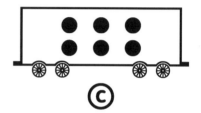

(C)

8.

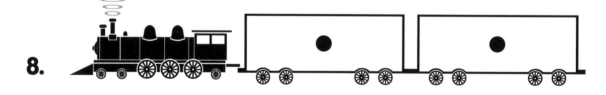

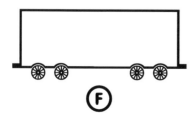

(F)

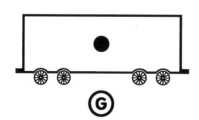

(G)

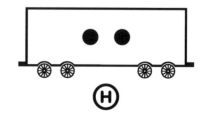

(H)

Number Puzzles

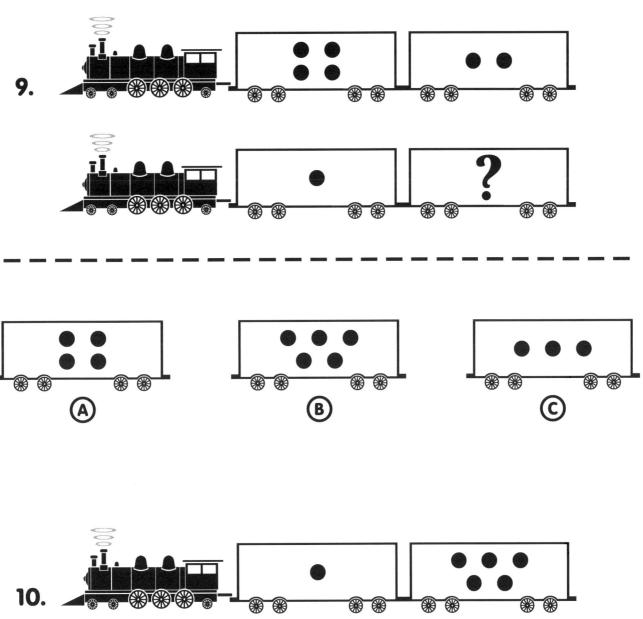

9.

A   B   C

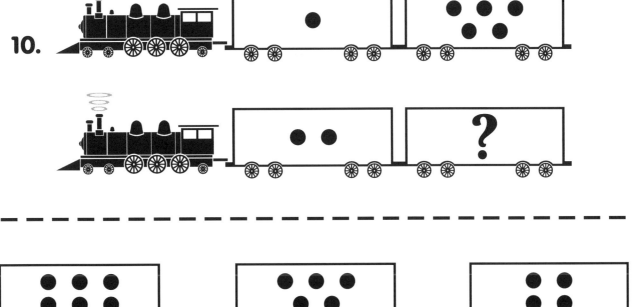

10.

F   G   H

Number Puzzles

11.

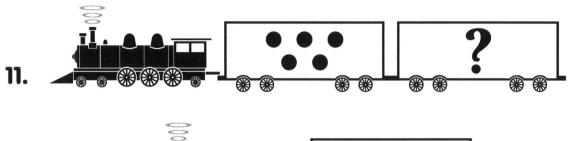

- -

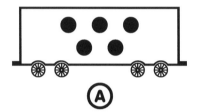

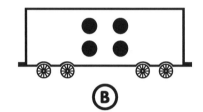

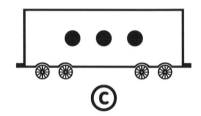

12.

- -

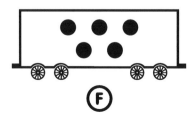

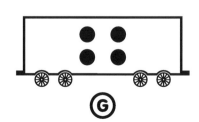

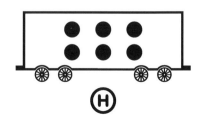

Number Puzzles

13.

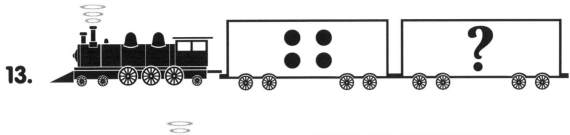

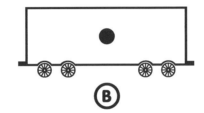 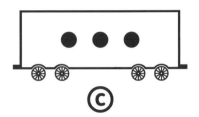

14.

  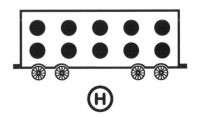

Directions:

The questions in this section are like the sample below:

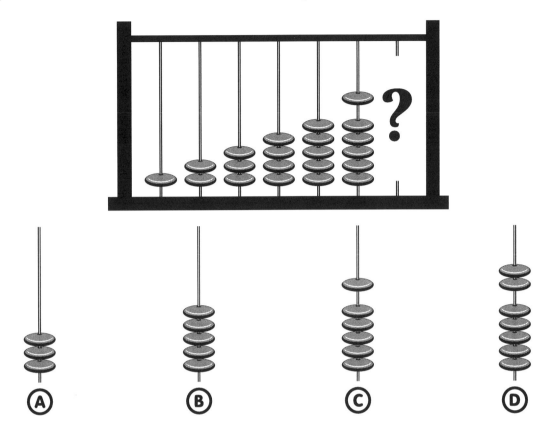

Look at the picture of the abacus. Look at the numbers of beads in each column. Think about the number pattern created by the columns of beads. Now look at the answer choices. Choose the answer that completes the number pattern. In this case the series is **1, 2, 3, 4, 5, 6**… The next number is obviously **7** so find the answer choice that shows **7 beads** (Notice that 7 is broken up into 5 beads and 2 beads).

Find the area marked Number Series on your answer sheet. Now find the S (sample) row. Since the answer is **7**, fill in the **D** space in row S.

Do all of the questions in this section in the same way (using the bubbles under each question or on the answer sheets, as your parents want). Try to answer each question.

Number Series

1.

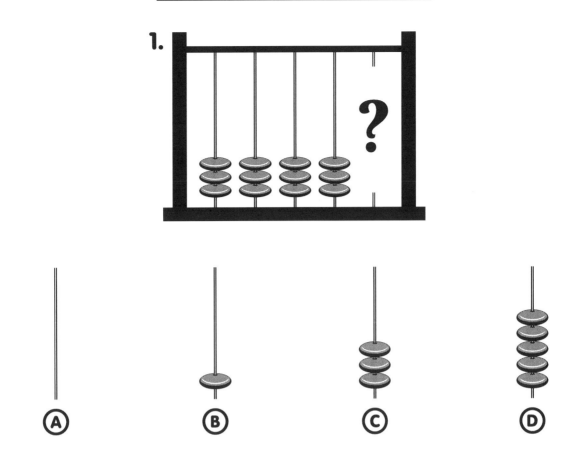

Ⓐ   Ⓑ   Ⓒ   Ⓓ

- -

2.

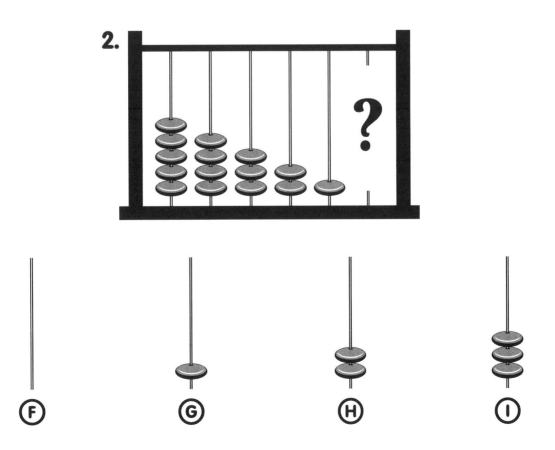

Ⓕ   Ⓖ   Ⓗ   Ⓘ

Number Series

3.

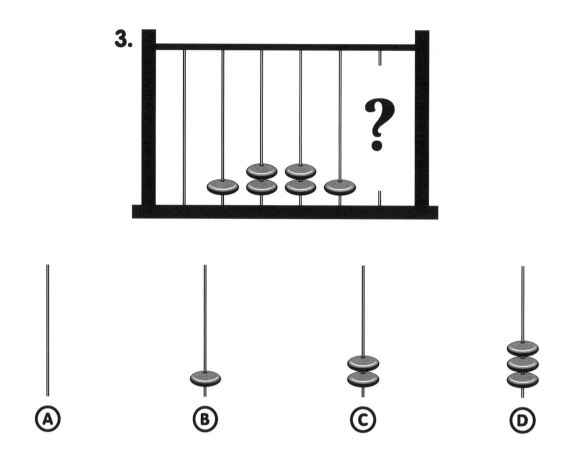

4.

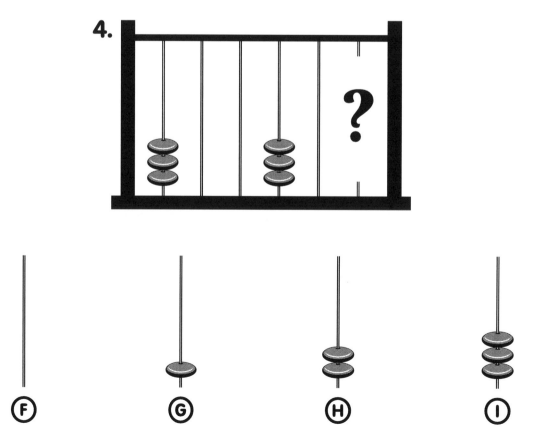

Big Brains Books - Crush the CogAT® Series - Practice Test 1

Number Series

5.

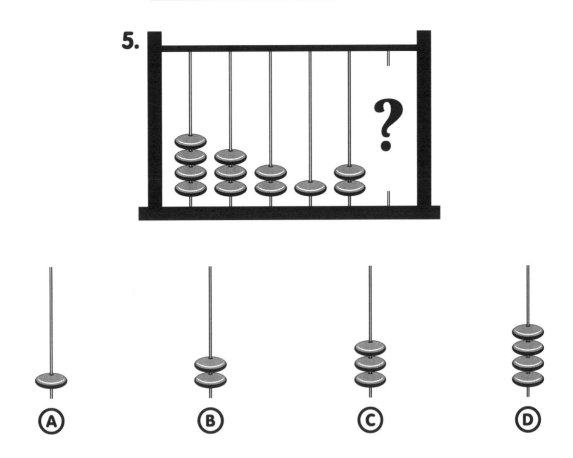

6.

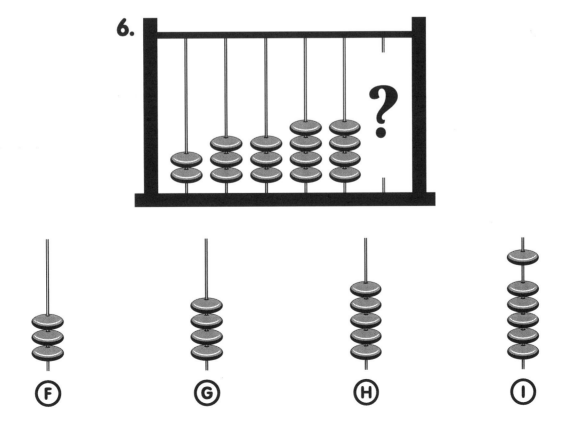

Number Series

7.

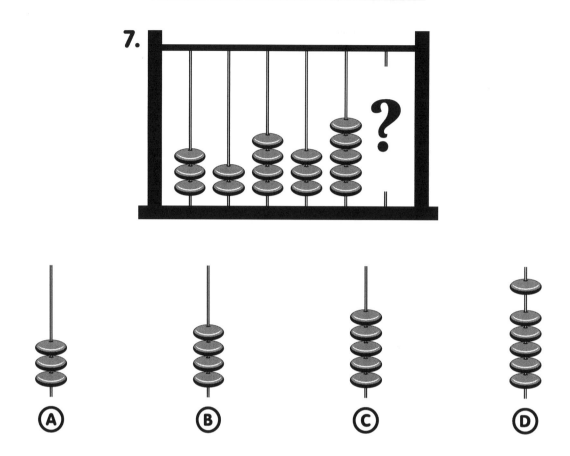

8.

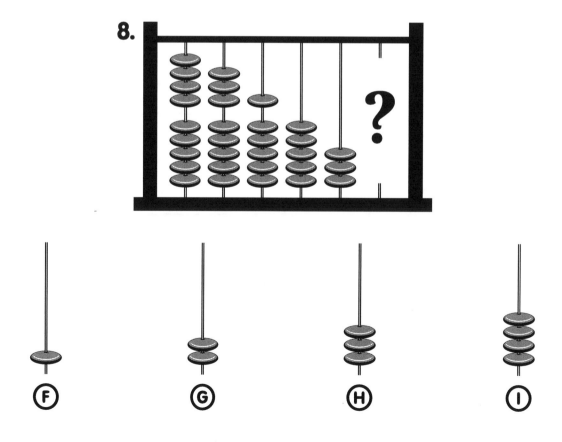

Big Brains Books - Crush the CogAT® Series - Practice Test 1

Number Series

9.

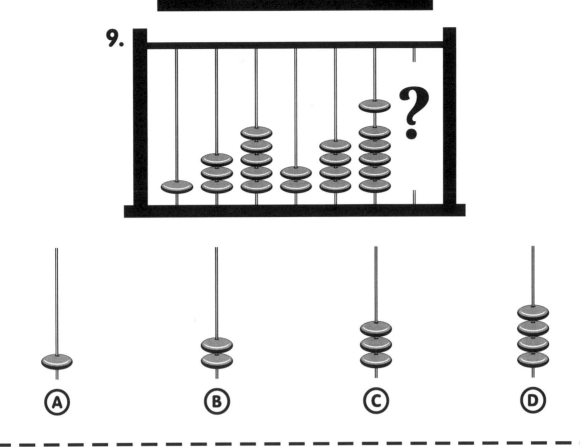

10.

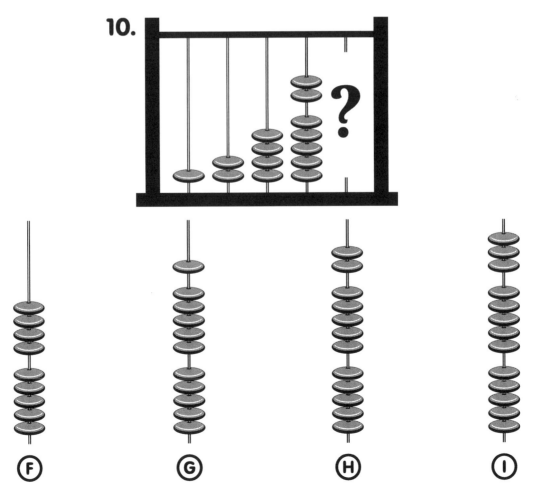

Number Series

11.

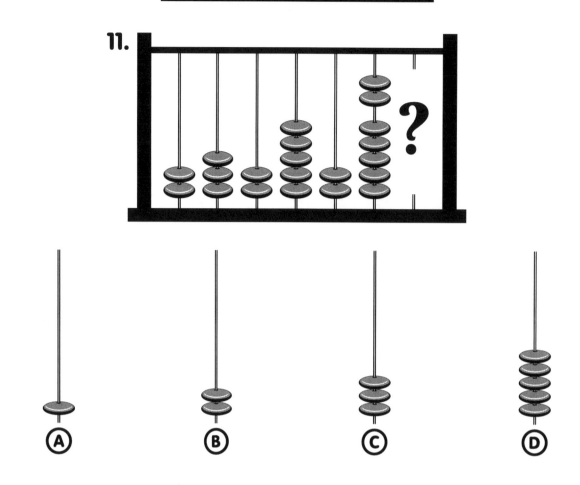

(A)   (B)   (C)   (D)

12.

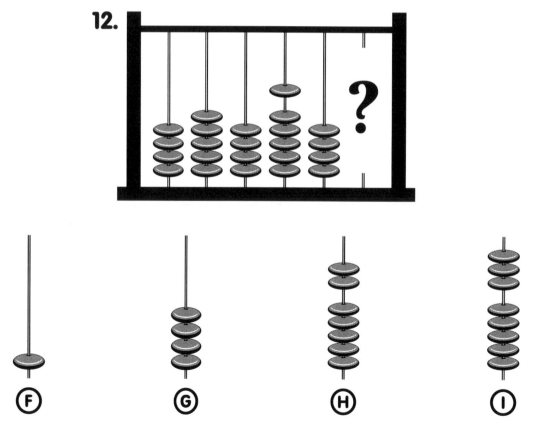

(F)   (G)   (H)   (I)

Number Series

13.

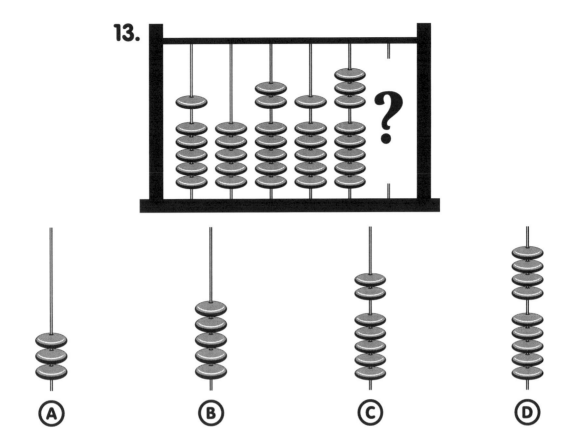

14.

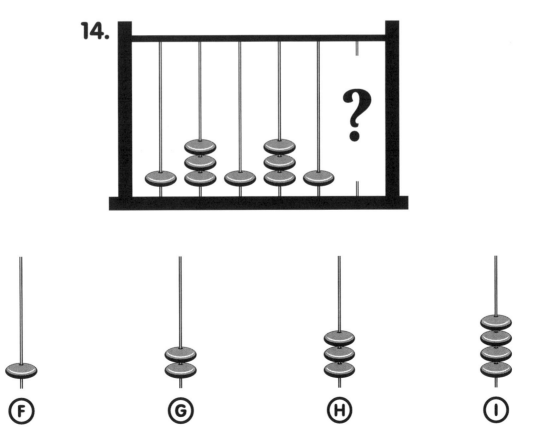

Number Series

15.

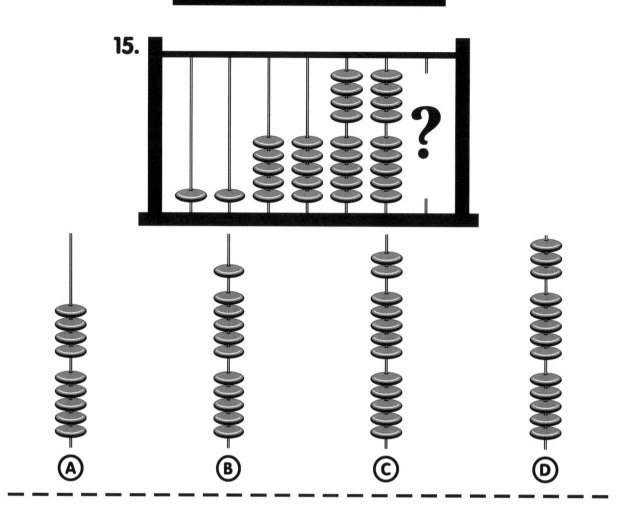

A **B** **C** **D**

16.

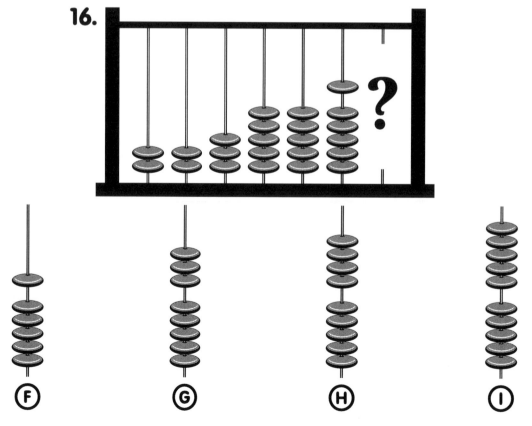

F **G** **H** **I**

Number Series

17.

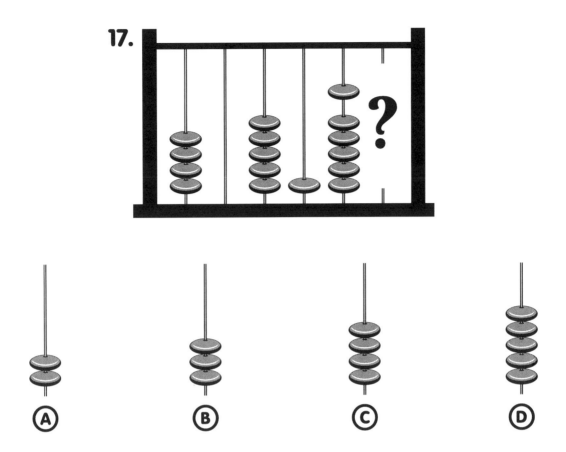

Ⓐ   Ⓑ   Ⓒ   Ⓓ

- -

18.

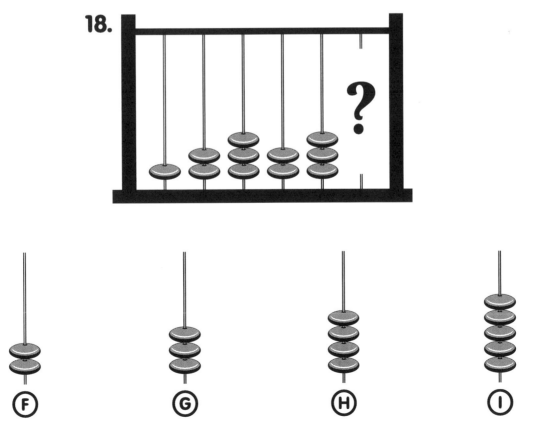

Ⓕ   Ⓖ   Ⓗ   Ⓘ

Directions:

The questions in this section are like the sample below:

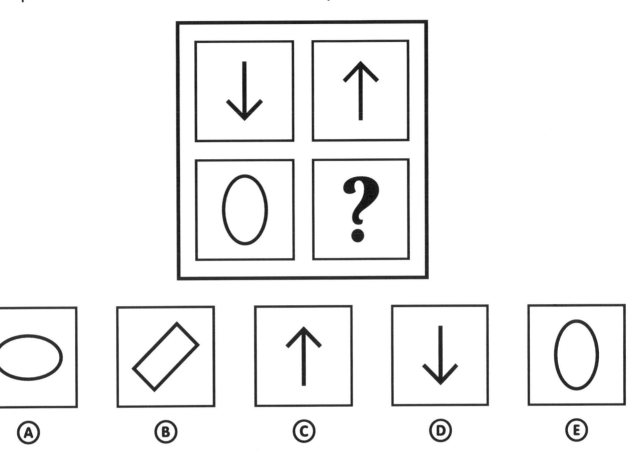

Look at the top two figures. Think about how they are related (Are they the same? Are they different in some particular way?) Now look at the lower figure. Which of the answer choices creates the same relationship with the lower figure as the two upper figures have together? In this case, the first arrow is **up**, then the second is **down**. The first oval is **up/down** and the final answer choice (could be) **down/up** (its flipped form is identical to unflipped).

Find the area marked Figure Matrices on your answer sheet. Now find the S (sample) row. Since the answer is the **oval**, fill in the **E** space in row S.

Do all of the questions in this section in the same way (using the bubbles under each question or on the answer sheets, as your parents want). Try to answer each question.

Figure Matrices

1.

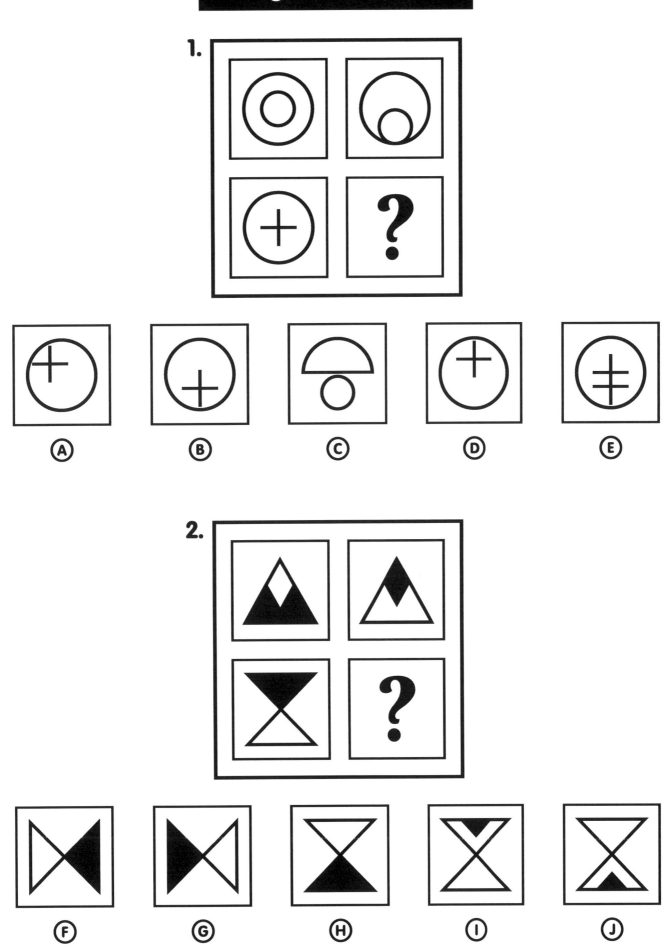

(A)   (B)   (C)   (D)   (E)

2.

(F)   (G)   (H)   (I)   (J)

Figure Matrices

3.

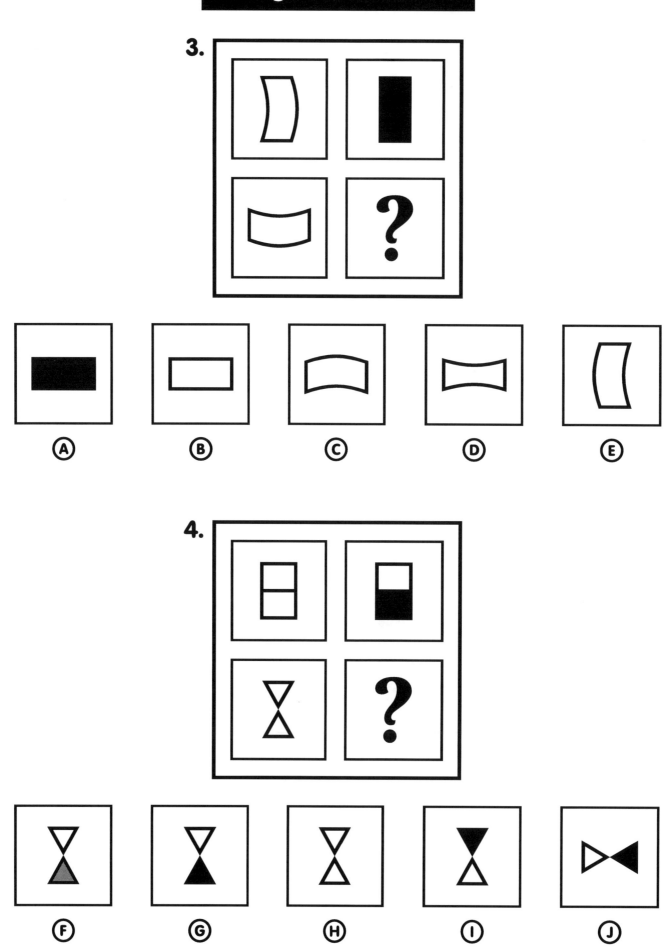

A B C D E

4.

F G H I J

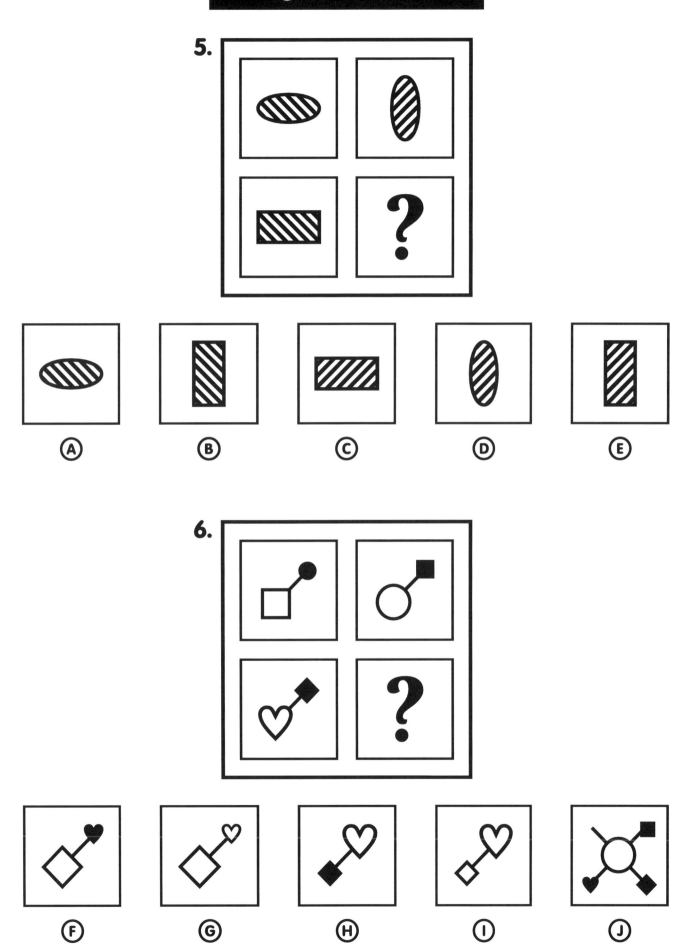

5.

Ⓐ   Ⓑ   Ⓒ   Ⓓ   Ⓔ

6.

Ⓕ   Ⓖ   Ⓗ   Ⓘ   Ⓙ

Figure Matrices

7.

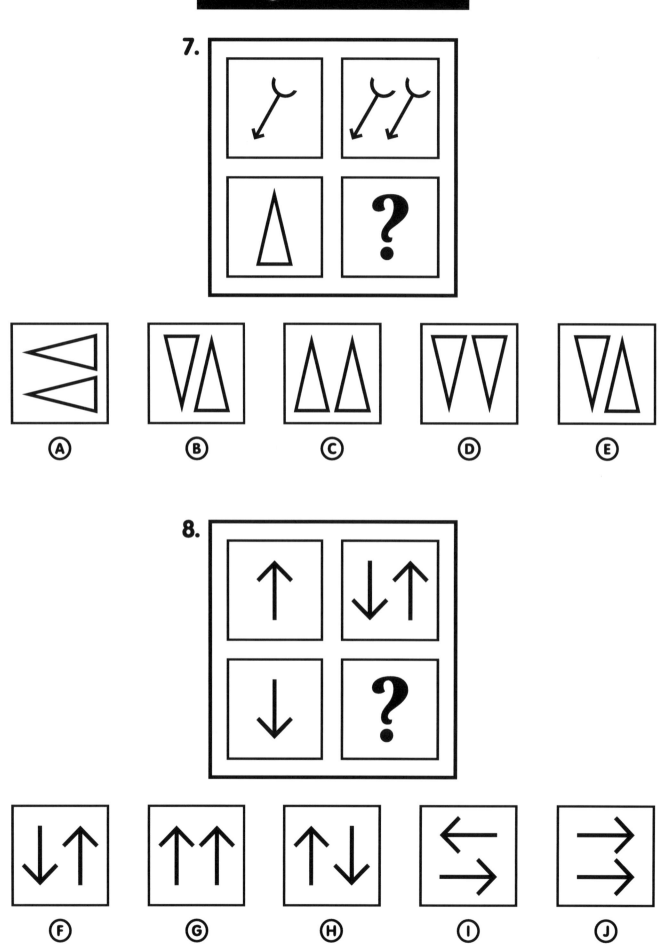

(A) (B) (C) (D) (E)

8.

(F) (G) (H) (I) (J)

Figure Matrices

9.

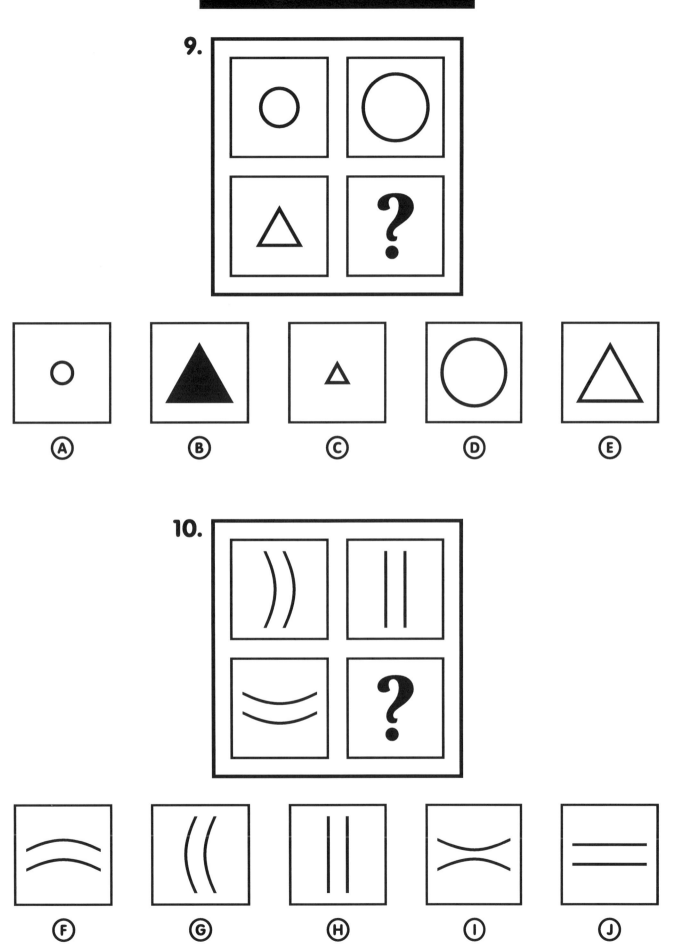

A   B   C   D   E

10.

F   G   H   I   J

Figure Matrices

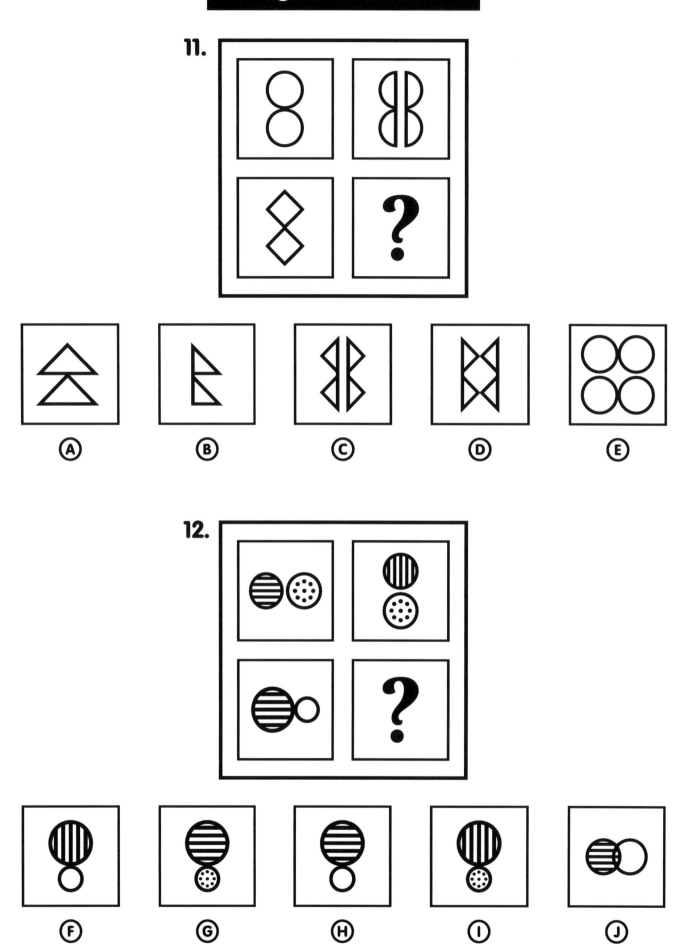

11.

A B C D E

12.

F G H I J

80   Big Brains Books - Crush the CogAT® Series - Practice Test 1

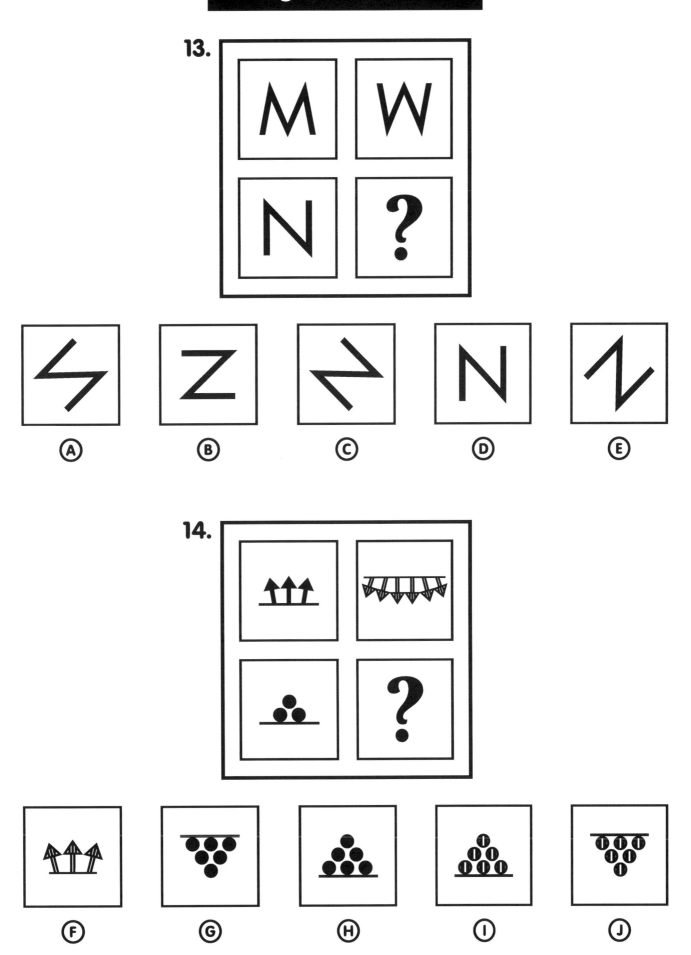

Figure Matrices

15.

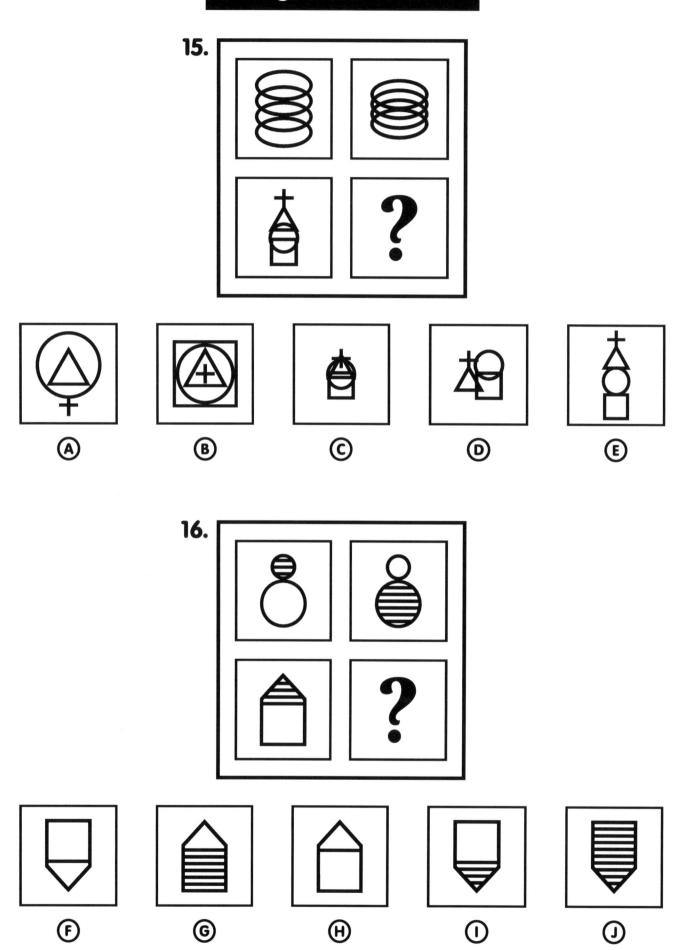

A   B   C   D   E

16.

F   G   H   I   J

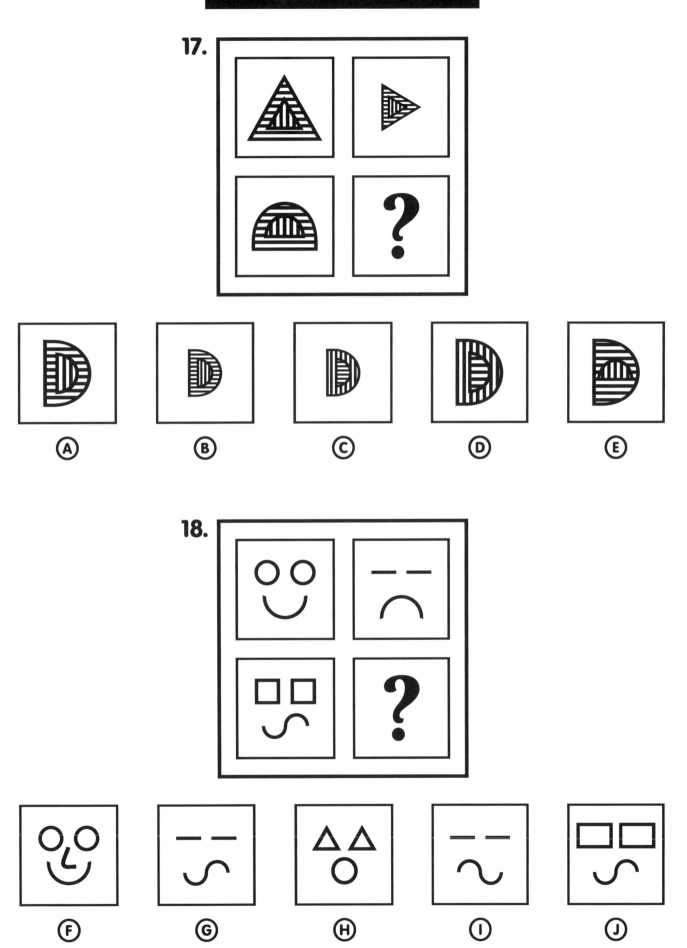

17.

Ⓐ   Ⓑ   Ⓒ   Ⓓ   Ⓔ

18.

Ⓕ   Ⓖ   Ⓗ   Ⓘ   Ⓙ

Directions:

The questions in this section are like the sample below:

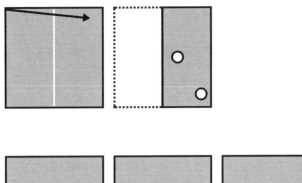

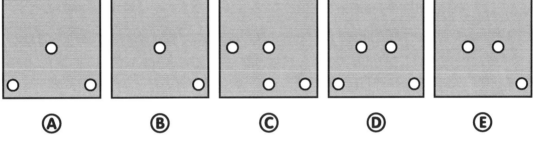

Look at the series of images. They show a piece of paper being folded then having holes punched through it. Think about what the paper will look like when it is unfolded. Fill in the bubble under the answer that shows what the paper will look like when it is unfolded. In this case, it's fairly obvious that the answer is **D**.

Find the area marked Paper Folding on your answer sheet. Now find the S (sample) row. Since the answer is **D**, fill in the **D** space in row S.

Do all of the questions in this section in the same way (using the bubbles under each question or on the answer sheets, as your parents want). Try to answer each question.

Paper Folding

1.

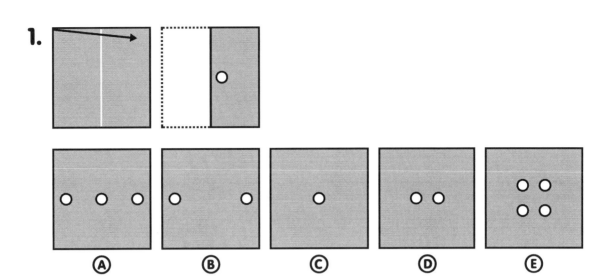

2.

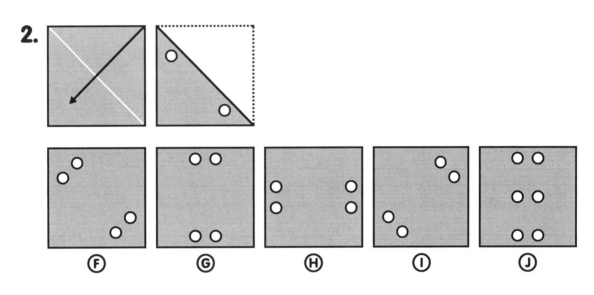

3.

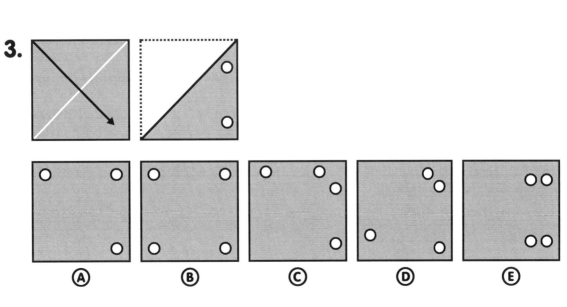

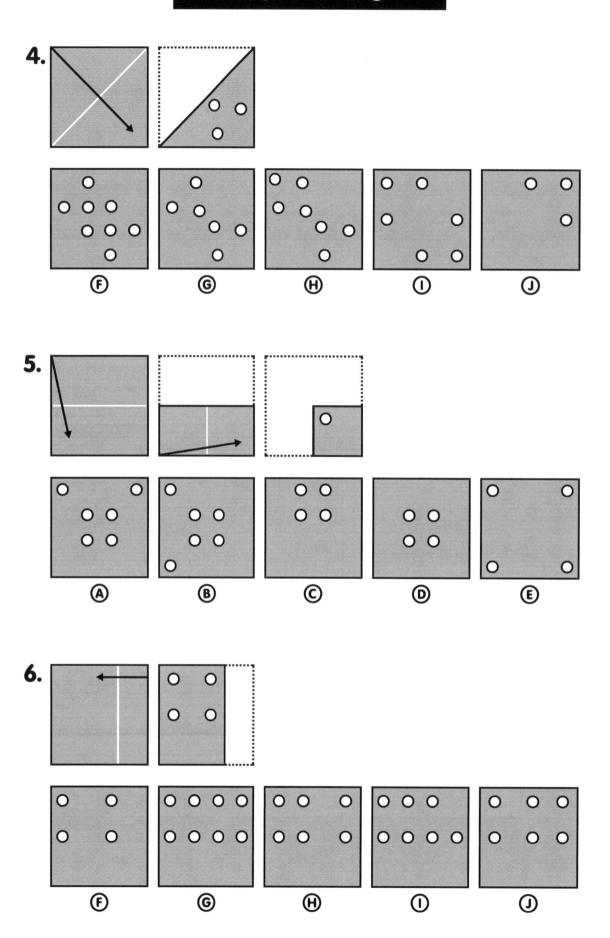

4.

5.

6.

7.

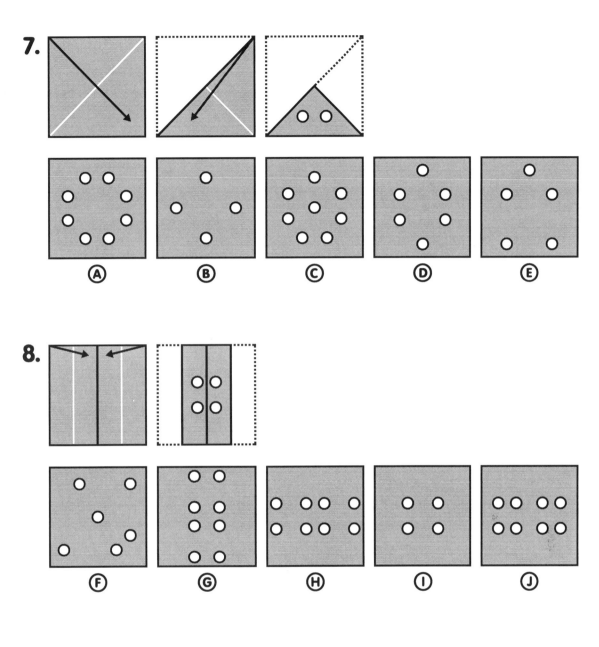

8.

9.

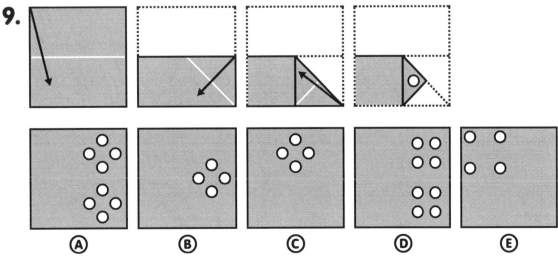

10.

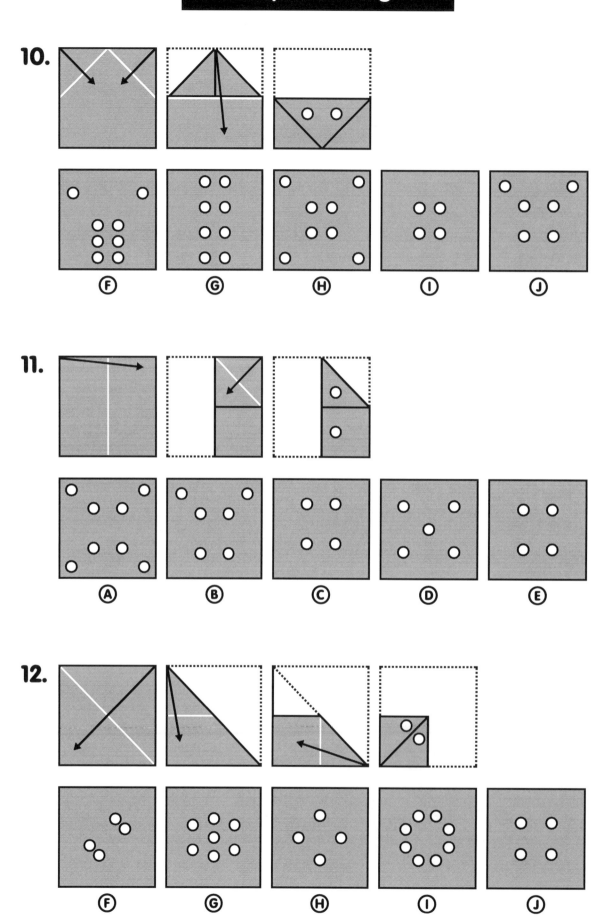

11.

12.

13.

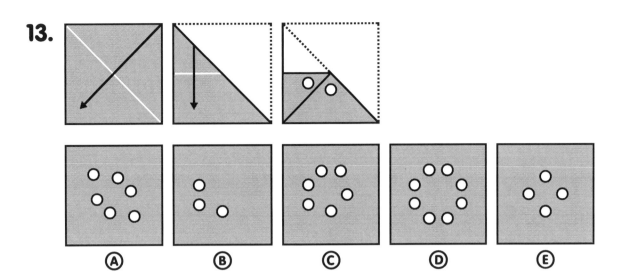

14.

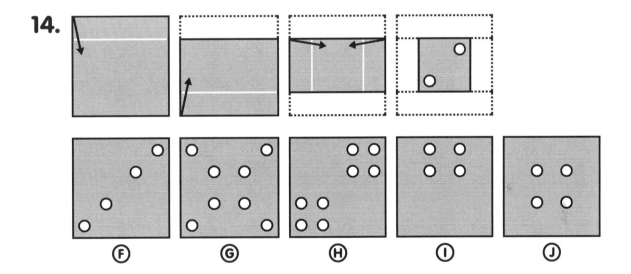

Figure Classification

Directions:

The questions in this section are like the sample below:

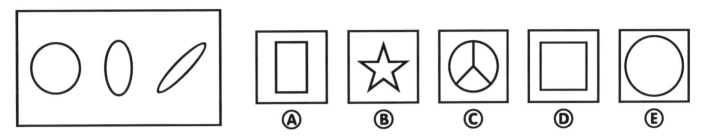

Look at the first three figures. Think about how they are the same. Now look at the answer choices and find the choice that belongs in the same group (that is the same as the three figures, in some way). Since all the original figures are **curved shapes**, we are looking for a **curved shape**. Clearly, answer choice **E** is the only curved shape (with nothing inside it).

Find the area marked Figure Classification on your answer sheet. Now find the S (sample) row. Since the answer is **E**, fill in the **E** space in row S.

Do all of the questions in this section in the same way (using the bubbles under each question or on the answer sheets, as your parents want). Try to answer each question.

Figure Classification

1.

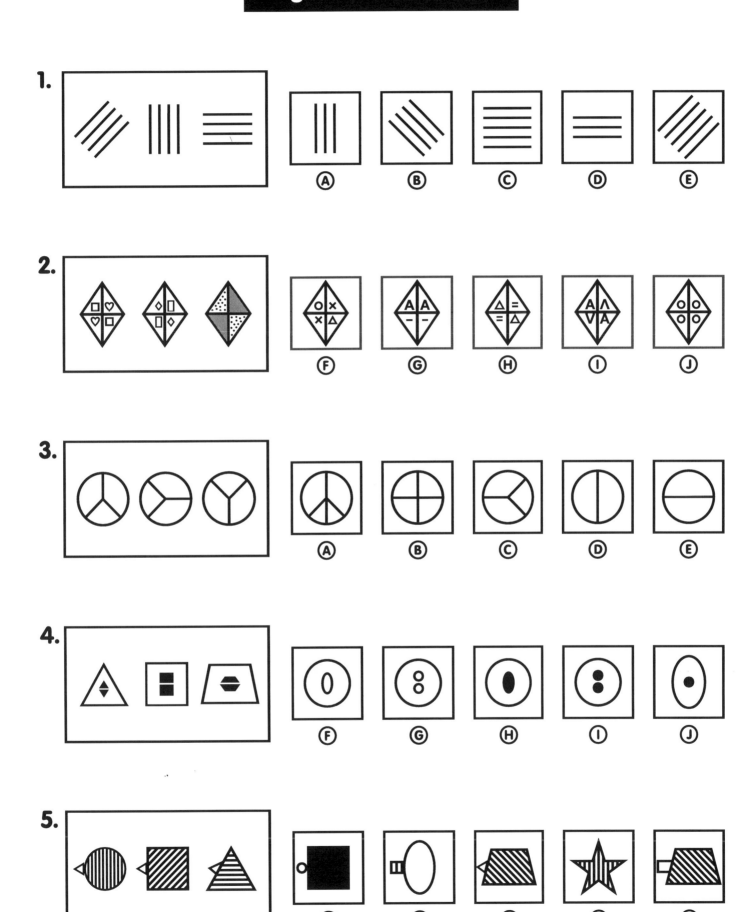

Figure Classification

6.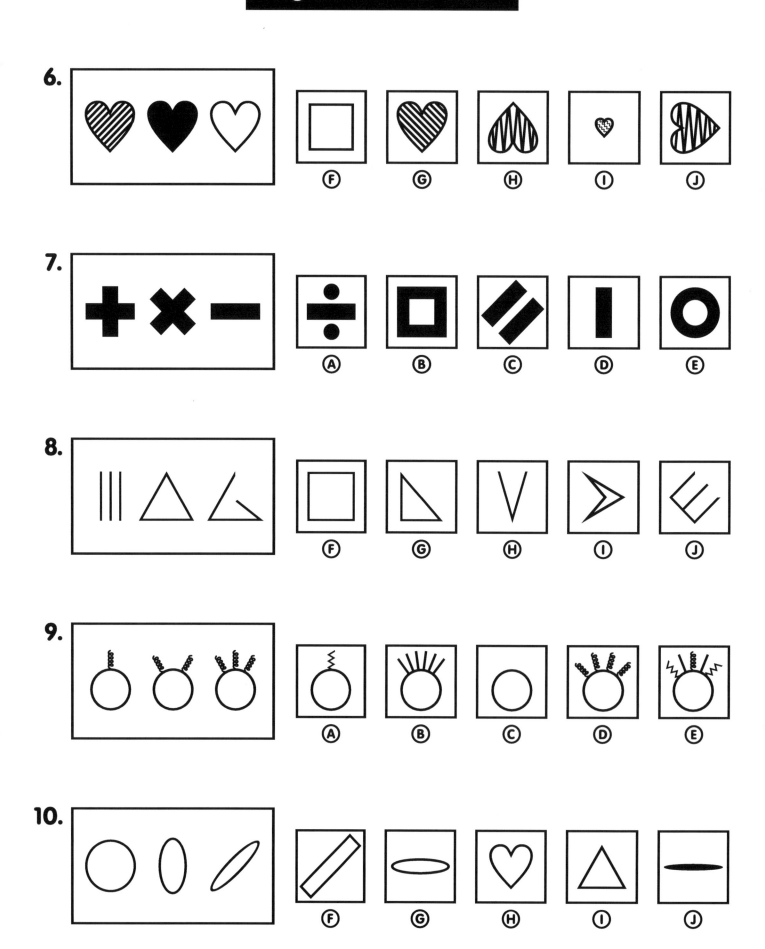

Big Brains Books - Crush the CogAT® Series - Practice Test 1

Figure Classification

11.

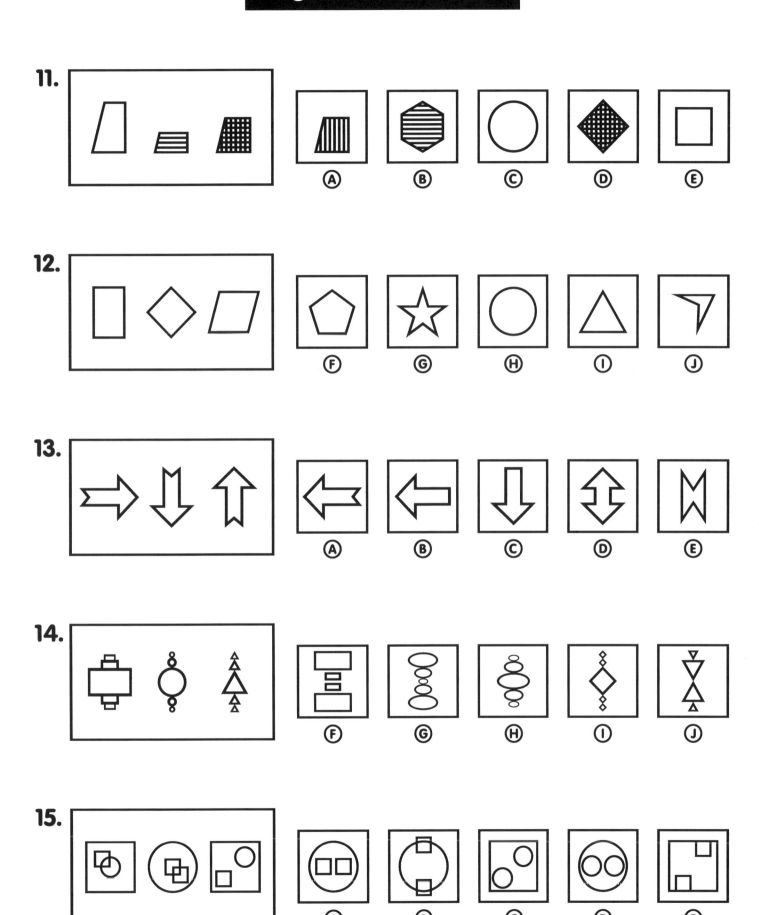

12.

13.

14.

15.

16.

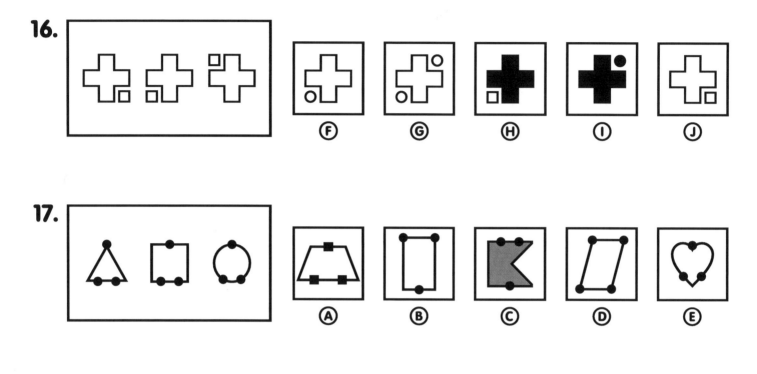

17.

18.

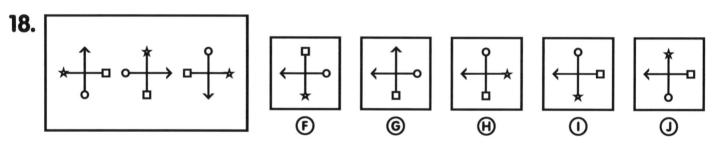

Answer Key

Picture Analogies

S. C

1. C	7. B	13. B
2. G	8. F	14. H
3. B	9. A	15. C
4. H	10. H	16. H
5. A	11. A	17. A
6. H	12. G	18. G

Sentence Completion

S. B

1. E	7. A	13. B
2. G	8. J	14. F
3. A	9. A	15. E
4. J	10. I	16. J
5. B	11. A	17. A
6. J	12. J	18. F

Picture Classification

S. C

1. A	7. A	13. A
2. H	8. G	14. H
3. A	9. C	15. C
4. H	10. H	16. H
5. C	11. C	17. C
6. H	12. F	18. F

Answer Key

Number Analogies

S. Ⓐ Ⓑ **Ⓒ**

1.	**Ⓐ**	Ⓑ	Ⓒ	7.	**Ⓐ**	Ⓑ	Ⓒ	13.	**Ⓐ**	Ⓑ	Ⓒ
2.	Ⓕ	**Ⓖ**	Ⓗ	8.	**Ⓕ**	Ⓖ	Ⓗ	14.	**Ⓕ**	Ⓖ	Ⓗ
3.	Ⓐ	Ⓑ	**Ⓒ**	9.	Ⓐ	Ⓑ	**Ⓒ**	15.	Ⓐ	**Ⓑ**	Ⓒ
4.	**Ⓕ**	Ⓖ	Ⓗ	10.	**Ⓕ**	Ⓖ	Ⓗ	16.	Ⓕ	Ⓖ	**Ⓗ**
5.	Ⓐ	**Ⓑ**	Ⓒ	11.	**Ⓐ**	Ⓑ	Ⓒ	17.	Ⓐ	Ⓑ	**Ⓒ**
6.	Ⓕ	**Ⓖ**	Ⓗ	12.	**Ⓕ**	Ⓖ	Ⓗ	18.	Ⓕ	**Ⓖ**	Ⓗ

Number Puzzles

S. **Ⓐ** Ⓑ Ⓒ

1.	**Ⓐ**	Ⓑ	Ⓒ	6.	Ⓕ	**Ⓖ**	Ⓗ	11.	Ⓐ	Ⓑ	**Ⓒ**
2.	Ⓕ	Ⓖ	**Ⓗ**	7.	Ⓐ	Ⓑ	**Ⓒ**	12.	Ⓕ	**Ⓖ**	Ⓗ
3.	**Ⓐ**	Ⓑ	Ⓒ	8.	**Ⓕ**	Ⓖ	Ⓗ	13.	**Ⓐ**	Ⓑ	Ⓒ
4.	Ⓕ	**Ⓖ**	Ⓗ	9.	Ⓐ	Ⓑ	**Ⓒ**	14.	Ⓕ	**Ⓖ**	Ⓗ
5.	Ⓐ	Ⓑ	**Ⓒ**	10.	Ⓕ	Ⓖ	**Ⓗ**				

Number Series

S. Ⓐ Ⓑ Ⓒ **Ⓓ**

1.	Ⓐ	Ⓑ	**Ⓒ**	Ⓓ	7.	Ⓐ	**Ⓑ**	Ⓒ	Ⓓ	13.	Ⓐ	Ⓑ	**Ⓒ**	Ⓓ
2.	**Ⓕ**	Ⓖ	Ⓗ	Ⓘ	8.	Ⓕ	**Ⓖ**	Ⓗ	Ⓘ	14.	Ⓕ	Ⓖ	**Ⓗ**	Ⓘ
3.	**Ⓐ**	Ⓑ	Ⓒ	Ⓓ	9.	Ⓐ	Ⓑ	**Ⓒ**	Ⓓ	15.	Ⓐ	Ⓑ	Ⓒ	**Ⓓ**
4.	**Ⓕ**	Ⓖ	Ⓗ	Ⓘ	10.	Ⓕ	**Ⓖ**	Ⓗ	Ⓘ	16.	Ⓕ	**Ⓖ**	Ⓗ	Ⓘ
5.	Ⓐ	Ⓑ	**Ⓒ**	Ⓓ	11.	Ⓐ	**Ⓑ**	Ⓒ	Ⓓ	17.	**Ⓐ**	Ⓑ	Ⓒ	Ⓓ
6.	Ⓕ	Ⓖ	**Ⓗ**	Ⓘ	12.	Ⓕ	Ⓖ	**Ⓗ**	Ⓘ	18.	Ⓕ	Ⓖ	**Ⓗ**	Ⓘ

Answer Key

Figure Matrices

S. A B C D **E**

1. A **B** C D E	7. A B **C** D E	13. A B C **D** E
2. F G **H** I J	8. F G **H** I J	14. F G H I **J**
3. **A** B C D E	9. A B C D **E**	15. A B **C** D E
4. F **G** H I J	10. F G H I **J**	16. F **G** H I J
5. A B C D **E**	11. A B **C** D E	17. A **B** C D E
6. **F** G H I J	12. **F** G H I J	18. F G H **I** J

Paper Folding

S. A B C **D** E

1. A B C **D** E	6. F G H I **J**	11. A **B** C D E
2. **F** G H I J	7. **A** B C D E	12. F G H **I** J
3. A B **C** D E	8. F G **H** I J	13. A B **C** D E
4. F **G** H I J	9. **A** B C D E	14. F G **H** I J
5. A B C **D** E	10. F G H I **J**	

Figure Classification

S. A B C D **E**

1. A **B** C D E	7. **A** B C D E	13. **A** B C D E
2. F G **H** I J	8. F **G** H I J	14. F G **H** I J
3. A B **C** D E	9. A B C **D** E	15. **A** B C D E
4. F G H **I** J	10. F **G** H I J	16. F G H I **J**
5. A B **C** D E	11. **A** B C D E	17. A B C D **E**
6. F **G** H I J	12. F G H I **J**	18. **F** G H I J

Answer Form

Picture Analogies

S. Ⓐ Ⓑ Ⓒ

1. Ⓐ Ⓑ Ⓒ
2. Ⓕ Ⓖ Ⓗ
3. Ⓐ Ⓑ Ⓒ
4. Ⓕ Ⓖ Ⓗ
5. Ⓐ Ⓑ Ⓒ
6. Ⓕ Ⓖ Ⓗ

7. Ⓐ Ⓑ Ⓒ
8. Ⓕ Ⓖ Ⓗ
9. Ⓐ Ⓑ Ⓒ
10. Ⓕ Ⓖ Ⓗ
11. Ⓐ Ⓑ Ⓒ
12. Ⓕ Ⓖ Ⓗ

13. Ⓐ Ⓑ Ⓒ
14. Ⓕ Ⓖ Ⓗ
15. Ⓐ Ⓑ Ⓒ
16. Ⓕ Ⓖ Ⓗ
17. Ⓐ Ⓑ Ⓒ
18. Ⓕ Ⓖ Ⓗ

Sentence Completion

S. Ⓐ Ⓑ Ⓒ Ⓓ Ⓔ

1. Ⓐ Ⓑ Ⓒ Ⓓ Ⓔ
2. Ⓕ Ⓖ Ⓗ Ⓘ Ⓙ
3. Ⓐ Ⓑ Ⓒ Ⓓ Ⓔ
4. Ⓕ Ⓖ Ⓗ Ⓘ Ⓙ
5. Ⓐ Ⓑ Ⓒ Ⓓ Ⓔ
6. Ⓕ Ⓖ Ⓗ Ⓘ Ⓙ

7. Ⓐ Ⓑ Ⓒ Ⓓ Ⓔ
8. Ⓕ Ⓖ Ⓗ Ⓘ Ⓙ
9. Ⓐ Ⓑ Ⓒ Ⓓ Ⓔ
10. Ⓕ Ⓖ Ⓗ Ⓘ Ⓙ
11. Ⓐ Ⓑ Ⓒ Ⓓ Ⓔ
12. Ⓕ Ⓖ Ⓗ Ⓘ Ⓙ

13. Ⓐ Ⓑ Ⓒ Ⓓ Ⓔ
14. Ⓕ Ⓖ Ⓗ Ⓘ Ⓙ
15. Ⓐ Ⓑ Ⓒ Ⓓ Ⓔ
16. Ⓕ Ⓖ Ⓗ Ⓘ Ⓙ
17. Ⓐ Ⓑ Ⓒ Ⓓ Ⓔ
18. Ⓕ Ⓖ Ⓗ Ⓘ Ⓙ

Picture Classification

S. Ⓐ Ⓑ Ⓒ

1. Ⓐ Ⓑ Ⓒ
2. Ⓕ Ⓖ Ⓗ
3. Ⓐ Ⓑ Ⓒ
4. Ⓕ Ⓖ Ⓗ
5. Ⓐ Ⓑ Ⓒ
6. Ⓕ Ⓖ Ⓗ

7. Ⓐ Ⓑ Ⓒ
8. Ⓕ Ⓖ Ⓗ
9. Ⓐ Ⓑ Ⓒ
10. Ⓕ Ⓖ Ⓗ
11. Ⓐ Ⓑ Ⓒ
12. Ⓕ Ⓖ Ⓗ

13. Ⓐ Ⓑ Ⓒ
14. Ⓕ Ⓖ Ⓗ
15. Ⓐ Ⓑ Ⓒ
16. Ⓕ Ⓖ Ⓗ
17. Ⓐ Ⓑ Ⓒ
18. Ⓕ Ⓖ Ⓗ

Answer Form

Number Analogies

S. Ⓐ Ⓑ Ⓒ

1. Ⓐ Ⓑ Ⓒ
2. Ⓕ Ⓖ Ⓗ
3. Ⓐ Ⓑ Ⓒ
4. Ⓕ Ⓖ Ⓗ
5. Ⓐ Ⓑ Ⓒ
6. Ⓕ Ⓖ Ⓗ

7. Ⓐ Ⓑ Ⓒ
8. Ⓕ Ⓖ Ⓗ
9. Ⓐ Ⓑ Ⓒ
10. Ⓕ Ⓖ Ⓗ
11. Ⓐ Ⓑ Ⓒ
12. Ⓕ Ⓖ Ⓗ

13. Ⓐ Ⓑ Ⓒ
14. Ⓕ Ⓖ Ⓗ
15. Ⓐ Ⓑ Ⓒ
16. Ⓕ Ⓖ Ⓗ
17. Ⓐ Ⓑ Ⓒ
18. Ⓕ Ⓖ Ⓗ

Number Puzzles

S. Ⓐ Ⓑ Ⓒ

1. Ⓐ Ⓑ Ⓒ
2. Ⓕ Ⓖ Ⓗ
3. Ⓐ Ⓑ Ⓒ
4. Ⓕ Ⓖ Ⓗ
5. Ⓐ Ⓑ Ⓒ

6. Ⓕ Ⓖ Ⓗ
7. Ⓐ Ⓑ Ⓒ
8. Ⓕ Ⓖ Ⓗ
9. Ⓐ Ⓑ Ⓒ
10. Ⓕ Ⓖ Ⓗ

11. Ⓐ Ⓑ Ⓒ
12. Ⓕ Ⓖ Ⓗ
13. Ⓐ Ⓑ Ⓒ
14. Ⓕ Ⓖ Ⓗ

Number Series

S. Ⓐ Ⓑ Ⓒ Ⓓ

1. Ⓐ Ⓑ Ⓒ Ⓓ
2. Ⓕ Ⓖ Ⓗ Ⓘ
3. Ⓐ Ⓑ Ⓒ Ⓓ
4. Ⓕ Ⓖ Ⓗ Ⓘ
5. Ⓐ Ⓑ Ⓒ Ⓓ
6. Ⓕ Ⓖ Ⓗ Ⓘ

7. Ⓐ Ⓑ Ⓒ Ⓓ
8. Ⓕ Ⓖ Ⓗ Ⓘ
9. Ⓐ Ⓑ Ⓒ Ⓓ
10. Ⓕ Ⓖ Ⓗ Ⓘ
11. Ⓐ Ⓑ Ⓒ Ⓓ
12. Ⓕ Ⓖ Ⓗ Ⓘ

13. Ⓐ Ⓑ Ⓒ Ⓓ
14. Ⓕ Ⓖ Ⓗ Ⓘ
15. Ⓐ Ⓑ Ⓒ Ⓓ
16. Ⓕ Ⓖ Ⓗ Ⓘ
17. Ⓐ Ⓑ Ⓒ Ⓓ
18. Ⓕ Ⓖ Ⓗ Ⓘ

Answer Form

Figure Matrices

S. Ⓐ Ⓑ Ⓒ Ⓓ Ⓔ

1. Ⓐ Ⓑ Ⓒ Ⓓ Ⓔ
2. Ⓕ Ⓖ Ⓗ Ⓘ Ⓙ
3. Ⓐ Ⓑ Ⓒ Ⓓ Ⓔ
4. Ⓕ Ⓖ Ⓗ Ⓘ Ⓙ
5. Ⓐ Ⓑ Ⓒ Ⓓ Ⓔ
6. Ⓕ Ⓖ Ⓗ Ⓘ Ⓙ

7. Ⓐ Ⓑ Ⓒ Ⓓ Ⓔ
8. Ⓕ Ⓖ Ⓗ Ⓘ Ⓙ
9. Ⓐ Ⓑ Ⓒ Ⓓ Ⓔ
10. Ⓕ Ⓖ Ⓗ Ⓘ Ⓙ
11. Ⓐ Ⓑ Ⓒ Ⓓ Ⓔ
12. Ⓕ Ⓖ Ⓗ Ⓘ Ⓙ

13. Ⓐ Ⓑ Ⓒ Ⓓ Ⓔ
14. Ⓕ Ⓖ Ⓗ Ⓘ Ⓙ
15. Ⓐ Ⓑ Ⓒ Ⓓ Ⓔ
16. Ⓕ Ⓖ Ⓗ Ⓘ Ⓙ
17. Ⓐ Ⓑ Ⓒ Ⓓ Ⓔ
18. Ⓕ Ⓖ Ⓗ Ⓘ Ⓙ

Paper Folding

S. Ⓐ Ⓑ Ⓒ Ⓓ Ⓔ

1. Ⓐ Ⓑ Ⓒ Ⓓ Ⓔ
2. Ⓕ Ⓖ Ⓗ Ⓘ Ⓙ
3. Ⓐ Ⓑ Ⓒ Ⓓ Ⓔ
4. Ⓕ Ⓖ Ⓗ Ⓘ Ⓙ
5. Ⓐ Ⓑ Ⓒ Ⓓ Ⓔ

6. Ⓕ Ⓖ Ⓗ Ⓘ Ⓙ
7. Ⓐ Ⓑ Ⓒ Ⓓ Ⓔ
8. Ⓕ Ⓖ Ⓗ Ⓘ Ⓙ
9. Ⓐ Ⓑ Ⓒ Ⓓ Ⓔ
10. Ⓕ Ⓖ Ⓗ Ⓘ Ⓙ

11. Ⓐ Ⓑ Ⓒ Ⓓ Ⓔ
12. Ⓕ Ⓖ Ⓗ Ⓘ Ⓙ
13. Ⓐ Ⓑ Ⓒ Ⓓ Ⓔ
14. Ⓕ Ⓖ Ⓗ Ⓘ Ⓙ

Figure Classification

S. Ⓐ Ⓑ Ⓒ Ⓓ Ⓔ

1. Ⓐ Ⓑ Ⓒ Ⓓ Ⓔ
2. Ⓕ Ⓖ Ⓗ Ⓘ Ⓙ
3. Ⓐ Ⓑ Ⓒ Ⓓ Ⓔ
4. Ⓕ Ⓖ Ⓗ Ⓘ Ⓙ
5. Ⓐ Ⓑ Ⓒ Ⓓ Ⓔ
6. Ⓕ Ⓖ Ⓗ Ⓘ Ⓙ

7. Ⓐ Ⓑ Ⓒ Ⓓ Ⓔ
8. Ⓕ Ⓖ Ⓗ Ⓘ Ⓙ
9. Ⓐ Ⓑ Ⓒ Ⓓ Ⓔ
10. Ⓕ Ⓖ Ⓗ Ⓘ Ⓙ
11. Ⓐ Ⓑ Ⓒ Ⓓ Ⓔ
12. Ⓕ Ⓖ Ⓗ Ⓘ Ⓙ

13. Ⓐ Ⓑ Ⓒ Ⓓ Ⓔ
14. Ⓕ Ⓖ Ⓗ Ⓘ Ⓙ
15. Ⓐ Ⓑ Ⓒ Ⓓ Ⓔ
16. Ⓕ Ⓖ Ⓗ Ⓘ Ⓙ
17. Ⓐ Ⓑ Ⓒ Ⓓ Ⓔ
18. Ⓕ Ⓖ Ⓗ Ⓘ Ⓙ

For Additional Practice

Crush the CogAT®- Practice Test 2

Made in the USA
San Bernardino, CA
12 August 2015